II0639140

Discovering
CATHEDRALS

David Pepin

With drawings by the author

Shire Publications Ltd

CONTENTS

The cover design of Lincoln Cathedral is by Ron Shaddock.

Copyright © 1977 by David Pepin. No. 112 in the 'Discovering' series. ISBN 0 85263 374 2. First published 1971, editions 1974 and 1977. All rights reserved. No part of this publication may be reproduced or transmitted in any form or by any means, electronic or mechanical, including photocopy, recording, or any information storage and retrieval system, without permission in writing from the publishers, Shire Publications Ltd., Cromwell House, Church Street, Princes Risborough, Aylesbury, Bucks., U.K.

1. INTRODUCTION

Certain of our cathedrals rank as architectural landmarks of the highest order, not only in Britain but also when they are compared with their counterparts in Europe. It could be said that each cathedral is unique and even the modest and less architecturally attractive ones often possess features and treasures which are unknown elsewhere.

Many people who visit these national shrines—and year by year more and more are joining their ranks—will naturally have their favourites. The author is conscious that, in a limited work such as this, many important things have been omitted and the reader's indulgence on this point would be appreciated. The aim of this book therefore is to give a modest introduction to an extremely complex subject.

It goes without saying that cathedrals are not museums. Whilst they embody much of great beauty and historical interest, first and foremost they are places of worship and ideally, centres of service, connected with people past and present. The beauty associated with the worship conveyed in the music, ceremonial and architecture, stems from a great Faith through the ages. Of course it is not wrong simply to enjoy the architecture, but to know *why* a church or cathedral was built in the first place adds to this enjoyment.

The building, therefore, is an expression of something deeper than the mere bricks and stones themselves. A cathedral is not an end in itself. Without people a cathedral is an empty shell. It is the faithful resident who worships in the place regularly, the many people on the staff who maintain the building in a host of ways and the casual worshipper and visitor, all these, who 'make it tick', who are its *raison d'etre*. Each cathedral has a distinct atmosphere, a personality. It is hoped that the following historical and architectural notes will enable the reader to come face to face with these personalities, and through his own experience, help him to 'discover' the cathedrals for himself.

A cathedral usually has an organisation known as 'The Friends' who have the welfare of the cathedral at heart and will always welcome other like-minded people as members. The author is grateful to such friends and others, both clergy and lay on the staffs of cathedrals, who have willingly helped him in his pursuit of exploring and discovering.

2. WHAT IS A CATHEDRAL?

A cathedral is the main church in a church district known as a diocese (in this case Anglican or Church of England) where the bishop of the diocese has his *cathedra* or throne. Cathedra is a word meaning chair. Hence the word *cathedral* for the special church. Usually the largest church in an area fulfills this function, with all that this entails in the way of special services, concerts, diocesan and children's festivals and events such as youth pilgrimages. There is also the daily round of worship even when very few people are present, but nonetheless, on behalf of the Christian family in the diocese. There are a few very small cathedrals, however, and also some very large abbeys of cathedral-like proportions, such as Westminster, Bath and Tewkesbury, which are not cathedrals. It is the bishop's cathedra alone that gives a church cathedral status, irrespective of size or historical importance.

The boundaries of many dioceses are at present under review. In the not too distant future we shall no doubt see the creation of more dioceses and the raising to cathedral status of yet more parish churches. At present there are forty-eight dioceses (and so forty-eight cathedrals) in England and Wales, the area covered by this book. Each diocese is made up of many parishes, each with its own parish clergy. Everyone in Britain has a parish church and a cathedral. In England there are two provinces, Canterbury and York. The former includes twenty-nine dioceses south of a line running from north Shropshire, Staffordshire, East Derbyshire, Leicestershire, Lincolnshire to the Humber. The thirteen dioceses north of the line come under the York province which also has its own archbishop, styled Primate of England although the Archbishop of Canterbury is Primate of *All* England. The Church in Wales covers six dioceses and has its own archbishop. Only the archbishops of Canterbury and York and the bishops of London, Durham and Winchester have permanent seats in the House of Lords. Twenty-one of the remaining bishops sit in the Upper House according to their dates of seniority as bishops.

A cathedral is run by a special staff of clergymen called a chapter, headed by a dean or provost. Contrary to general belief, it is not the bishop of the diocese who is in direct charge of his cathedral church and its affairs. Among the many lay people (non clergy) who are also on the staff, the architect and permanent mason obviously have vital jobs to

4

do. The master of the choristers, the head organist, trains the choir of men and boys. There are still over thirty cathedral choir schools educating boys in music as well as in the subjects of a normal school curriculum. Not all cathedrals have choir schools but they nonetheless still succeed in maintaining a high musical standard, an essential part of cathedral worship. Such cathedrals usually have choirs made up of boys who attend ordinary schools during the day, as opposed to cathedral choir schools which are residential.

Origins of cathedrals

Certain cathedrals were once part of monasteries. When Henry VIII closed down these establishments in the 1530s (The Dissolution) such cathedrals were refounded by the king and given a new status, staffed by a dean and chapter rather than by a prior and monks. The last prior often became the first dean. They became cathedrals of the 'New Foundation'. The ones so affected were **Canterbury, Carlisle, Durham, Ely, Norwich, Rochester, Winchester and Worcester.**

To these were added a few more churches which had never been cathedrals but which were part of monasteries, staffed by an abbot and monks. The last abbot usually became the first dean of the 'New Foundation'. Cathedrals of this type are **Bristol, Chester, Gloucester, Oxford and Peterborough.**

Some cathedrals were never part of monastic establishments (although the existence of cloisters often gives the impression that they were). They are known as cathedrals of the 'Old Foundation' run by a body of clergy known as canons. The canons were often called secular, that is 'of the world', as opposed to monks who were of a closed order in a monastery. This group comprises **Bangor, Chichester, Exeter, Hereford, Lichfield, Lincoln, Llandaff, London (St. Paul's), St. Asaph, St. David's, Salisbury, Wells and York.**

Certain cathedrals received their status comparatively recently. They were parish churches or specially endowed churches called collegiate churches. Today some of these are known as parish church cathedrals. Here is the list of cathedrals of 'Modern Foundation' beginning with the year 1836: **Ripon, Manchester, St. Albans, Truro, Liverpool, Newcastle, Southwell, Wakefield.** Of this century: **Southwark, Birmingham, Chelmsford, St. Edmundsbury, Sheffield, Coventry, Bradford, Newport (Monmouth), Brecon, Blackburn, Leicester, Derby, Guildford, Portsmouth.** Most of these are run by a provost and chapter as opposed to a dean and chapter. These new cathedrals were founded in areas where industry and population were on the increase. Although often referred to as 'national shrines', our cathedrals are not financed (as yet) by the state. Widespread appeals are often necessary to preserve these great buildings, without which our land would undoubtedly be the poorer in countless ways, difficult to measure in financial terms. After all, what is a cathedral, a church, or any work of art for that matter, *worth?*

A cathedral is really the highest expression of the art of man in Western Europe. It is essential for our generation, in seeking to further the greater glory of God, to use these great buildings imaginatively for the welfare of people everywhere; the worshippers, the admirers and the many people who have not perhaps, as yet, discovered the full potential of these vital centres of Christian witness.

3. IT WAS NOT BUILT IN A DAY!

There are various styles or periods of architecture which overlap considerably and it is difficult to say exactly when one style ends and another begins. They differ in expression from one country to another, even one district to another. For the purpose of this book we shall be thinking mainly of the architectural styles of Britain of the past 900 years.

The term Gothic appears a great deal. It applies to the styles of architecture of the thirteenth to sixteenth centuries. The Goths were a barbaric people who ravaged Europe 1500 years ago, destroying the ancient world and its learning and bringing in the Dark Ages of the history text books. The word Gothic was used only a few hundred years ago to describe the architecture of four to seven hundred years ago which, although remarkable and beautiful to us now, was at one time considered 'barbaric', different and unlike the ancient classical styles of Greece and Rome which had withstood the tests of time.

When the average person has a mental picture of a cathedral it is usually in the Gothic style. The period we call the Middle Ages, when the Gothic cathedrals were built, was indeed 'the cathedral age' just as this is the 'machine age'. Stone was *the* material. The mason and his craft became highly respected, and we still admire and preserve the work of these great craftsmen. Cathedrals and churches are still built today but not in the great numbers they were in the period from about 1000 to 1500.

As we travel through the country we are never far away

from a church, abbey or cathedral. To understand styles of architecture we need to go and look, to explore, to discover for ourselves. A cathedral is a remarkable 'visual aid'. Any one of our main British cathedrals can display a wide variety of styles since it was probably built, enlarged, often illtreated, lovingly and unlovingly restored over hundreds of years. Nevertheless there is a unity, an artistry and, usually, a happy compromise in the blending of the styles, which is typically British.

Looking for clues

We have seen that styles vary from age to age. Elements in style, moreover, often arose out of the need to solve real problems. Vaulting with stone ribs was developed as an alternative to the wooden roofs which, in Norman churches, were constant fire risks. Indeed, many did go up in flames. In course of time vaults became more and more elaborate in design and more and more daring in construction (see page 12). The buttress was devised to give support to walls.

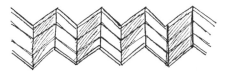

NORMAN ROMANESQUE. CHEVRON or ZIG-ZAG

A FEW OF THE MOST COMMON

MOULDINGS TO LOOK OUT FOR...

EARLY ENGLISH PERIOD — DOG-TOOTH
FOUR LEAVES SET PYRAMID-FASHION.
AT CERTAIN ANGLES THEY APPEAR LIKE A DOG'S TEETH

14th Century
BALL-FLOWER
and
FOLIAGE

GROUND PLAN SHOWING THE LAYOUT AND
FEATURES OF A TYPICAL CATHEDRAL

1	West Front	13	Central Tower—Crossing
2	West Door	14	North Transept
3	Western towers	15	South Transept
4	Nave	16	Various chapels—on both sides of the building
5	Nave aisles		
6	Nave Arcade—arches and pillars		
7	Nave Altar	17	Presbytery
8	Choir Screen or Pulpitum	18	High Altar—the main altar
9	Choir Stalls	19	Eastern Transepts
10	Cathedra—The Bishop's Throne	20	Retro-choir—shrine or tomb of patron saint
11	Choir aisles	21	Lady Chapel
12	Presbytery aisles	22	Chapter House
		23	Cloister Walk

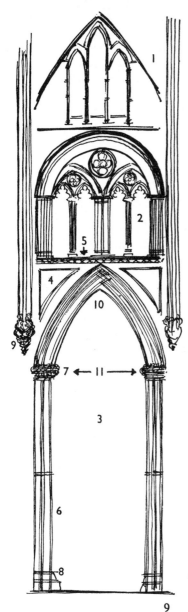

1 Clerestory
or Clearstorey,
where light enters

2 Triforium
or 'Blind Storey'

3 Main Arcade

4 Spandrel

5 Moulding

6 Shafts of pillars

7 Capital, often
elaborately carved

8 Base of column

9 Corbel, often
beautifully carved

10 Crown of arch

11 Span of arch

Note: These features
do not all
necessarily
appear
together.

*Special features of
British cathedrals in
general (when compared,
say, with those of
France) include their
setting within a close,
great length as opposed
to height, and splendid
central towers.*

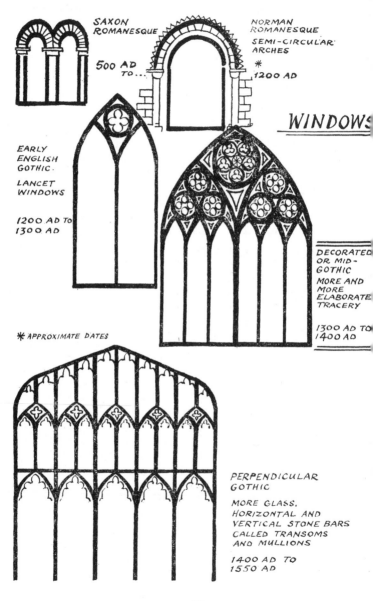

SAXON ROMANESQUE

500 AD TO...

NORMAN ROMANESQUE

SEMI-CIRCULAR ARCHES

* 1200 AD

WINDOWS

EARLY ENGLISH GOTHIC.

LANCET WINDOWS

1200 AD TO 1300 AD

DECORATED OR MID-GOTHIC

MORE AND MORE ELABORATE TRACERY

1300 AD TO 1400 AD

* APPROXIMATE DATES

PERPENDICULAR GOTHIC

MORE GLASS, HORIZONTAL AND VERTICAL STONE BARS CALLED TRANSOMS AND MULLIONS

1400 AD TO 1550 AD

10

MASSIVENESS
BOLD ZIG-ZAG
OR CHEVRON
PATTERN

DOORS

PILLARS

&ARCHES

POINTED
ARCHES

UNORNAMENTED
EARLY STAGE
OF GOTHIC

PURBECK
MARBLE OFTEN
USED

POINTED
ARCHES

ELABORATE
CARVING ON
CAPITALS
AND CORBELS

ARCHES STILL POINTED
BUT SOMEWHAT FLATTENED.
RECTILINEAR 'SQUARE' SHAPE

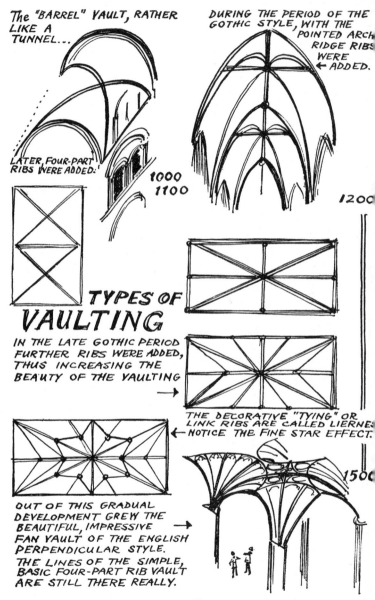

The "BARREL" VAULT, RATHER LIKE A TUNNEL...

LATER, FOUR-PART RIBS WERE ADDED.

1000
1100

DURING THE PERIOD OF THE GOTHIC STYLE, WITH THE POINTED ARCH RIDGE RIBS WERE ← ADDED.

1200

TYPES OF VAULTING

IN THE LATE GOTHIC PERIOD FURTHER RIBS WERE ADDED, THUS INCREASING THE BEAUTY OF THE VAULTING →

THE DECORATIVE "TYING" OR LINK RIBS ARE CALLED LIERNES ← NOTICE THE FINE STAR EFFECT.

1500

OUT OF THIS GRADUAL DEVELOPMENT GREW THE BEAUTIFUL, IMPRESSIVE FAN VAULT OF THE ENGLISH PERPENDICULAR STYLE. THE LINES OF THE SIMPLE, BASIC FOUR-PART RIB VAULT ARE STILL THERE REALLY. →

12

Windows offer many clues as to the period when a church was built. Saxon and Norman churches had thick walls and windows were at first really nothing more than slits, as in a castle. Windows gradually grew in size until the very walls themselves became 'walls of glass' (see page 10).

Mouldings also help to date a building (see page 7).

---

4. PLAIN AND SIMPLE

Saxon Romanesque architecture

Most people know that the Greeks and Romans were erecting grand buildings over 2000 years ago. Following the evacuation of Roman armed forces from Britain soon after A.D. 400 this country was plunged into a period of upheaval when almost every vestige of civilisation was destroyed or left to decay. These were the Dark Ages, which lasted over 500 years. Surprisingly, however, this was also the time of the great heroes of the Christian Church, and the reign of Alfred the Great was notable for its revival of art and learning. Monasteries were the guardians of learning. Monks and nuns worshipped and worked for the welfare of people, but few of their Saxon churches remain. Their style of building is called Saxon Romanesque, because it used the Roman rounded arch, as does the later Norman style which followed. Churches were based on the Roman basilica with rounded eastern apse. Very few Saxon Romanesque features remain in our cathedrals. At **St. Albans** where there was probably a Saxon church of considerable size, the little Saxon pillars, or balusters, can be seen at the transept crossing. Incidentally, at St. Albans the Norman tower is faced with pink tiles from the Roman town of Verulamium nearby and almost as old as Christianity itself. Much of the fabric here at St. Albans is from the deserted Roman town.

Beneath **Ripon** cathedral is a Saxon crypt unique among crypts, the oldest part of any British cathedral. The Saxon church built by Bishop Wilfrid was said to be one of the finest stone buildings in northern Europe. It was destroyed by Viking pirates but the crypt, built for the display of sacred relics, has survived and can still be visited today.

Saxon work can be detected in several places if one looks carefully. More often than not, however, it has been heavily disguised or covered up with more recent work. In most places where there is a great church or cathedral standing today there is evidence of a Christian church of some kind on the site from Saxon times.

5. STRENGTH AND FORTITUDE

Norman architecture

The Normans, led by Duke William, conquered England in 1066 and in the years immediately following, but prior to this several fine churches of no mean size had been built here by Norman masons. (There had already been considerable cultural traffic between Britain and Europe.) However, there is no doubt about it, that the Norman building drive after 1066 was tremendous and it left its permanent mark on the architectural scene. A very large number of cathedrals have Norman Romanesque work somewhere. First and foremost is **Durham** cathedral, the finest and least spoiled Norman Romanesque church in Europe. By 1133, after only about forty years of building, the cathedral had been completed. The superb nave pillars with their bold incised patterns make an unforgettable impact as one enters. The Norman church ended in an apse, as was the normal custom then, but at Durham, as in most places, the cathedral was later enlarged eastwards. This fine, massive church on its impressive site above the horseshoe loop of the river Wear, has three great towers. The two western ones, Norman at lower level, were later increased in height, as was the central tower.

At **Peterborough,** the least spoiled of great Norman churches after Durham, the curved apse behind the high altar remains. The eye is led to it along the impressive sweep of the Norman nave arcade, the choir, central tower, transepts and presbytery. The absence of any screen across the church makes for a unique uninterrupted view eastwards.

Norwich, too, still possesses its Norman apse with radiating chapels—the *chevet* as in a French church. In the whole of Europe, moreover, there are few cathedrals in which the once traditional placing of the bishop's throne at the centre of the apse, east of the high altar, remains to this day. Norwich cathedral takes pride of place in this respect. Subsequent architectural additions blend well with the Norman core (plate 6). The central tower, with a spire added later, has attractive Norman decoration.

Ely, Peterborough and **Norwich** all have similar long naves and the three churches are without crypts. The nave at Ely is also most impressive. This most beautiful cathedral, once called the Norman Lady as opposed to the Norman Lord at Durham, is built, surprisingly, on solid rock, in the flat marshy fenlands. The fascinating carving round the outside of the prior's door is a superb example of Norman Romanesque art.

As far as crypts are concerned, whilst there are fine ones at **Canterbury, Gloucester, Rochester** and **York,** the most notable is at **Worcester** with its forest of pillars all part of the original Norman church. Here there is an early example of a central pillar with several arches radiating from it, an idea that appeared later in the Worcester Chapter House, the forerunner of many circular or polygonal chapter houses with central pillars. The chapter house and vestibule at **Bristol** are especially good examples of Norman work and have a wealth of decoration.

At **Gloucester** and **Hereford** there are cylindrical pillars, a marked feature of Norman building in the west country (plate 15). The Hereford pillars and arches are late Norman with some very elaborate carving. Original Norman work is also still to be seen in the south transept here. At **Winchester** it is in the north transept where the solid fortress-like Norman architecture particularly impresses, especially when one considers that the great church was built on a raft of logs in a marsh! The Norman nave is still really there, too, but unseen! One cannot but wonder at the way in which the later Gothic builders here completely encased the Norman structure in a Gothic covering instead of pulling down and rebuilding as, for example, at **Canterbury.**

The first central tower at **Winchester** collapsed in 1107 and had to be replaced, but at **St. Albans** the tower, built of Roman bricks and tiles, is a fine example of Norman strength (plate 5). Central towers are a marked feature of British cathedrals. Almost all our cathedrals have one. This is not the case abroad. **Exeter,** an exception, has retained her Norman towers, one on each side of the church at the transept crossing, and this is unusual. The superb Norman tower at **Bury St Edmunds** stands apart from the cathedral since it was also originally the gateway in front of the now ruined abbey. It has been described as the finest Norman building in Britain.

The Norman Romanesque style, solid looking and massive, aptly conveyed the strength and fortitude of the Christian Church but, as far as architecture was concerned, there was to be what one might call a 'thaw'. This was gradual and in some places until late in the twelfth century building was still progressing in the Norman style. As early as 1096, however, only thirty years after the Conquest, the earliest stone-rib vaulted ceiling was built at Durham. A hundred years after this daring and momentous advance the pointed arch was really gaining ground so that in the late 1100s the beginnings of Gothic architecture, the Norman Transitional, appear in Britain. Examples of this change-over style are at **Canterbury, Ripon, Rochester** and **Worcester.**

More Norman architecture can be seen at: Canterbury, Carlisle, Chester, Chichester, Lincoln, Llandaff, Newport, Norwich, Oxford, Rochester, St Albans, St David's and Southwell.

---

6. GRACE AND ELEGANCE

Early English Gothic

In 1140 in France an occasion of great significance heralded in the Gothic style. The foundation stone of the new abbey church of St. Denis, on the outskirts of Paris, was laid in that year. Abbot Suger, the designer of St. Denis, wanted people to be uplifted in heart and mind and to this end he designed a church of great beauty and of great richness in decoration.

The Gothic style evolved in the region around Paris known as the Ile de France. The pointed arch was not an entirely new invention since it was known in the Middle East, but its introduction into European architecture profoundly affected the atmosphere of church buildings. In contrast to the Norman or Romanesque church where the emphasis is horizontal and 'down to earth', the Gothic church is designed to draw the eyes of the worshipper upwards. Wall space is smaller in area to allow for more and greater windows to let in plenty of light. Pillars become more and more slender, extremely tall clusters of stone rods, supporting high soaring arches and daring vaulted ceilings.

Soon after the murder of Thomas Becket in 1170 in his own cathedral at **Canterbury** and after a fire there, work was started on the rebuilding of the eastern end of the cathedral to house a shrine to the archbishop. In the true international spirit characteristic of the Church in those days, a French architect, William of Sens, was signed on for the task. After an unfortunate scaffolding accident which left him a cripple, he had to hand the work over to another William, an Englishman. The shrine of St. Thomas has since been removed but the choir and Trinity Chapel remain, early examples of the Gothic style in Britain.

The earliest expression of Gothic architecture in this

country is usually called Early English and it covers approximately the period 1200 to 1300. Architects and builders in England began to develop their own ideas and styles and three cathedrals that demonstrate this change are Wells, Salisbury and Lincoln.

At **Wells** the building of the cathedral in the Early English style was begun about 1180 and continued for about sixty years. The nave pillars have a very solid look about them, by no means Norman, of course, but nevertheless the clusters of slender shafts form quite massive piers (plate 14).

In 1220 at Old Sarum, the original Norman settlement at **Salisbury,** Bishop Poore (to appear later at Durham) obtained permission to move the Christian community away from the unpleasant and cramped site near the castle to a lower level on the banks of the river Avon where water was more plentiful. The cathedral at New Sarum was built for the most part according to the original design and within the short period of just under forty years in the Early English Gothic style. Certain parts, including the world-famous spire, were built later (plate 1). In the nave there is an abundant use of Purbeck marble (seen earlier at Canterbury) helping to produce a very clearly defined and bright atmosphere. The lancet style of window can be seen throughout the building and as such it is typical of this early Gothic style in England.

In 1192 Bishop Hugh from Avalon in France, supervised the start of the rebuilding of **Lincoln** cathedral, but his influence, though tremendous, was short-lived because he died before the turn of the century. (The Norman cathedral had been left in a ruinous condition by a freak earth tremor in April 1185.) Other equally competent people carried on the work after Bishop Hugh, notably Bishop Robert Grosseteste. The eastern end of the cathedral was built in the form of a *chevet,* French style, but this was later replaced by the famous Angel Choir with its beautiful carvings including the endearing Lincoln imp. Purbeck marble, shipped from Dorset, was extensively used throughout the building.

As far as west fronts are concerned notable Early English ones other than those at Salisbury and Wells are at Peterborough and Ripon. At **Peterborough,** where the west front is kept perpendicular to the Norman building by giant steel rods within the thick walls, there are three 80 feet high arches forming a unique and magnificent facade (plate 16). The **Ripon** west front is much smaller and somewhat plain, the marked feature here being the characteristically Early English lancet windows. Pride of place, however, is taken by the west front at **Wells,** the finest in the country, nearly 150 feet wide, comprising an impressive panorama of statues. There are prophets, saints, kings, and other carvings to instruct the medieval worshipper (and not least his twentieth century counterpart). Several of the figures are life-size and even larger, but unfortunately many are now in a damaged state as is the figure of Christ in Majesty high in the centre.

Just as Norman architecture of the eleventh and twelfth centuries had embodied the aspirations of the Church Militant, so Gothic architecture of the thirteenth century and after conveys the feeling of release and *joie de vivre* the aspirations of a Church Triumphant. In a Gothic church one cannot but be uplifted. For the thirteenth century worshipper confronted by such beauty, heaven had really come down to earth.

Features of the Early English period can also be seen as follows: Brecon, Bristol, Chichester, Ely, Hereford, Rochester, St Albans, St David's, Southwark, Worcester and York (note especially here the tall Early English lancet windows 'The Five Sisters' at the transept crossing).

Note: Westminster Abbey (not a cathedral). New work with marked French influence was carried out at the time of Henry III on this royal church. That was in the mid 1200s and it is interesting that the north transept at Hereford resembles parts of the abbey.

---

7. ENRICHMENT AND SPLENDOUR

Mid-Gothic or Decorated

It is difficult to imagine fully the original beauty of many of Britain's churches. Damage caused by image breakers and restorers has often ruined the original impact which these must have had on local worshippers and pilgrims. For the most part we are deprived of the gilding and the colour of church interiors.

Exeter cathedral is our finest 'decorated' cathedral (plate 2). The nave is not very high since its height was determined by the twin Norman towers at the transepts which were incorporated into the new building. The splendid vaulted ceiling has been likened to branching trees and it is continuous from west to east, a distance of three hundred feet. With no central tower to break the continuity it is thus unique and one of the finest cathedral roofs and certainly the longest unbroken Gothic vault in the world. With a pair of binoculars one can see more effectively the beautifully carved ceiling bosses which were designed to cover the meeting points of the ribs in vaulting. Vaulting, with its additional little link-up ribs called liernes, and bosses are both notable features of the Decorated style. At Exeter in fact all around there is elaborate, delicate carving in corbels and bosses and expert craftsmanship in wood and stone. The window tracery—patterns formed by stone work—is also a product of this period and both the east and west windows at Exeter are fine examples of this. Window tracery became more and more beautiful and complex during the Decorated period.

It is **Carlisle** cathedral, however, which possesses what is justly claimed to be the finest traceried window in England. It is very large and forms a superb eastern climax to the choir and high altar. The tracery of the east window immediately above the high altar at **Ripon** is also very fine. The West Window at **York** Minster is aptly called 'The Heart of Yorkshire', dating from 1338. The nave here is also in the Decorated style, and incidentally it is the widest and highest in England. Except in the side aisles there is unfortunately no stone vault. The chapter house is vast, with notable geometrical traceried windows and many weird and wonderful carvings on the stall canopies. It is an all the more wonderful building when one realises that, for all its size, there is no central pillar. A stone vault was intended but a wooden roof was built instead.

Among stone carvings, undoubtedly some of the finest of the period are those which adorn the smaller chapter house at **Southwell Minster,** Nottinghamshire's village cathedral. There are birds and animals among foliage—the famous 'Leaves of Southwell', a superb example of mediaeval craftsmanship.

Work on the nave at **Worcester** was interrupted by the Black Death and the demands of the French wars and so there are pillars in the Decorated style on one side and later Gothic on the other side, when work was resumed.

A staggering achievement of these years was accomplished at **Ely** cathedral, namely the erection of its unique wonder, the Octagon—the only Gothic dome and one of the most incredible engineering feats of the Middle Ages (plate 3). This was built in 1332 to replace a central Norman tower which had fallen in a storm ten years before. The oak structure supports four hundred tons of wood and lead. Eight oak corner posts, each over sixty feet high, form the framework of the Lantern which seems almost to hang above our heads. The Lady Chapel at Ely is also a very remarkable building, possessing the widest vaulted ceiling of the period, a gentle curve nearly fifty feet across. If only we could still see this unique chapel in all its original colour and beauty in windows and sculpture, but it is unfortunately one of those many places that suffered at the hands of Civil War soldiery.

At **Salisbury** in the mid 1300s, work on the central tower continued and the spire was built to top it all, to a height of just over four hundred feet, a mammoth achievement considering a total weight of 6400 tons is at stake! At **Lincoln** there was once a spire on the central tower, itself the highest tower of the Middle Ages in England (just over 270 feet) and with the spire it reached a height of nearly 525 feet, the tallest in Europe. A storm in the mid 1500s put paid to that.

By the first half of this century also the very high Lady Chapel at **Lichfield** was completed to rehouse the shrine of Saint Chad. The west front dates from about 1300 and the three famous spires, unique to Lichfield and familiarly known as the Ladies of the Vale (plate 7), originated in this Decorated period but these and the rest of the building have been considerably restored. The Lady Chapel at **Wells** and its subsequent link-up with the rest of the cathedral by means of a retro-choir beyond the high altar, is extremely beautiful. This Lady Chapel has an unusual octagonal shape with one of the finest lierne vaults. The retro-choir with its slender Purbeck marble shafts was built perhaps for a shrine, following the fashion of the time, but a local saint was not forthcoming! This reminds us that most of the extensive building drive of these years was made possible by money given by pilgrims. This was the age of pilgrimages and some cathedrals were more fortunate in the way of tombs, shrines and relics than others. Nevertheless work went on apace at Wells linking the eastern extension with the choir and presbytery which was also rebuilt in this century. The east window, the Golden Window above the high altar, is one of the finest in England. This part of Wells cathedral, with its feeling of light and space, is more characteristic of the Perpendicular style which was to follow towards the end of the century.

The beautiful chapter house at **Wells,** reached by climbing a unique flight of steps, was completed in the early 1300s. It has a superb vault radiating from a slender central pillar. The geometrical windows are decorated with the ball-flower ornamentation. Such mouldings are common in the Decorated style of the fourteenth century. In the nave the famous inverted arches of scissor design in the form of a cross (perhaps reminding us of Saint Andrew, the patron saint of the cathedral) were inserted about 1340 to strengthen the central tower. This tower is, for the most part, of the Decorated Gothic period.

It is on the exterior of the central tower at **Hereford** (plate 13) that the use of ball-flower adornment is so pronounced. We have seen that central towers are a vital and prominent feature of almost all English cathedrals, and the fourteenth and fifteenth centuries saw the building or rebuilding of most of them as money came in from visiting pilgrims. This is the case at Hereford where contributions offered during pilgrimages to the shrine of St. Thomas Cantelupe enabled the building of the fine central tower. There will be more about central towers in the next chapter, but it should be mentioned that the Decorated towers of the fourteenth century were originally designed to have spires which have since disappeared.

In the early 1370s work was started at **Gloucester** cathedral on renovating the cloisters. As yet this was not a cathedral but here we meet for the first time the earliest fan-vault of any note. The fan-vault was to be a highlight of the next style of architecture which was to develop within the following 150 years or so.

The fourteenth century was no easy time to live because the Hundred Years War with France began (1337) and the dreaded plague, the Black Death (1348-9) spread across Europe killing thousands and halving the population in some parts of England. It took its toll of craftsmen and labourers and held up building operations on many a church and cathedral. In spite of these seemingly obvious setbacks, however, we have seen that this century was notable for many remarkable achievements in architecture and in its embellishment with exquisite carving in wood and stone and elaborate window tracery. Such great works of art were once described as 'poems in stone'.

In addition to the examples already mentioned in this chapter, the following cathedrals possess notable work of the Decorated period: Bristol, Chester, Chichester, St Albans, St Asaph, St David's and Winchester.

8. SPACE AND LIGHT

Late Gothic: The Perpendicular style

The finest total expressions of the Perpendicular style are not to be found in cathedrals at all. The chapel of King's College in Cambridge is the best example, and numerous parish churches up and down the country are built in the style. **St Edmundsbury** cathedral is largely a Perpendicular church but with a modern extension of which more will be said later. Many wonderful parish churches of the period can be seen in the Cotswolds and East Anglia. Both these districts were noted for their sheep farming and its allied trades. England's trade in wool grew in importance during the latter part of the Middle Ages. The Black Death caused landowners to turn to sheep farming since labour was short and only a few men were needed to care for the flocks. The sheep farmers and wool merchants became very rich. In the towns they built many fine houses and most important of all, they spent vast sums of money on building and furnishing some very beautiful churches, many of which are of cathedral-like proportions. Some, like Cirencester parish church, are called 'cathedrals' in the figurative sense. Appropriately one wool merchant had these words set in stained glass: *I thank my God and ever shall, it is the sheep hath paid for all.*

The Perpendicular style is the third phase of Gothic architecture in England. It was also an English invention, peculiar to this country. While European architecture became more and more flamboyant, often with extreme adornment, in England the new style was clean cut, restrained and lofty. Another appropriate name for the style is rectilinear. Under the hands of ever daring architects and masons churches became frameworks of stone with extensive window areas filled with stained glass. The style appeared first in London, and then work began at Gloucester.

It was mentioned in the last chapter that the fan-vault appeared in the new cloisters at **Gloucester** in the 1370s. Even earlier than this work had started on the redesign of the Norman east end, beginning with the south transept. Fortunately for the monks of the then Abbey of St. Peter the cost was met by pilgrims' offerings received at the tomb of King Edward II murdered at Berkeley Castle in 1327 and buried in the abbey. The lierne vault over 90 feet up, the vertical tracery, the lofty mullions or pillars separating the windows and the great windows themselves, transformed the Gloucester choir and presbytery into a building full of space and light. The great east window, the largest of its kind in Britain, is now just over 600 years old and contains much of its original glass. Further east still is the delightful Lady Chapel, linked to the main church by the Whispering Gallery, a cleverly contrived bridge. The ambulatory still follows the earlier Norman plan. The work of transforming the choir and presbytery necessitated the insertion of the 'flying arches' at the central tower. The exterior of this 225 foot tower, also in the Perpendicular style of a later date, has an extremely fine appearance.

It is the central tower at **Worcester** that is the most impressive exterior feature there (plate 11). Completed in 1374 it really is at the cathedral's centre and this is unusual! It is the earliest of the Perpendicular towers, probably a forerunner of the Gloucester tower though not so high. The famous central tower at **Canterbury,** the Bell Harry, was built over a hundred years later at the end of the fifteenth century. The lantern of this tower has a magnificent fanvault. At Norman **Durham** the central tower was increased in height. The work began in 1465. About two thirds of the way up there are battlements, probably intended to be the top of an earlier design, but which now seem out of place. At the time of writing extensive engineering, restoration and archaeological work is under way to save **York** Minster from collapse. This is now the largest cathedral of the Middle Ages in Britain. It is the central tower, the largest in floor area in England, which has been the main source of anxiety here. The three towers date from the second half of the fifteenth century. It is unfortunate that the centre one, completed in 1480, lacks the usual corner pinnacles on the exterior, but the newly restored lantern stonevault, with nearly one hundred bosses, is quite breathtaking.

Ceiling bosses and vaults are two notable features of Perpendicular architecture, and **Norwich** cathedral has some of the finest examples. Here the Norman nave received its high vault in the 1460s (plate 6). Work on vaulting the rest of this great Norman church continued for many years. There are hundreds of bosses dotted throughout the vault and in the cloisters. Norwich has a pleasing blend of Norman and late Gothic, especially at the eastern end where there are tall Gothic windows, and flying buttresses on the exterior. There is added light and a sense of space here, the Norman building being much enhanced by the additional work.

Three major works of the Perpendicular period are the naves at Canterbury and Winchester and the choir at York. At **Canterbury** the superb Perpendicular nave replaces the earlier Norman one. Here are the familiar tall, slender pillars and pointed arches comprising one of the greatest architectural splendours of the late Middle Ages. It is interesting to compare this nave with the one at **Winchester.** Here again are soaring pillars and arches but there is a very basic difference. At Winchester the Norman structure is still there, but it has been encased in a Perpendicular style covering. Bishop William of Wykeham, founder of New College Oxford and St Mary's College Winchester, was a famous national figure of the fourteenth century and he was largely responsible for the work here at Winchester although subsequent bishops had a hand in the task as well. Wykeham is commemorated in one of the many chantry chapels for which the cathedral is famous.

Work on the choir at **York** began in the early 1360s. Lofty and full of light, this eastern end culminates in a great wall of glass. The east window is the largest of its kind still complete with its brilliant glass, made by John Thornton of Coventry in the early 1400s in only three years. The roof of this easternmost end is of wood imitating stone, and this is not the original, but a replacement, due to fire damage in the last century arising out of a reckless act by a mad fire-raiser.

It is perhaps the fan-vault, another ingenious and highly decorative invention of the Perpendicular architects, that leaves the most lasting impressions of delight and wonder. We have already seen that the fan-vault made its earliest appearance in the **Gloucester** cloisters. Over a hundred years later, in 1496, the 'new building' beyond the Norman apse at **Peterborough** was started. Its Perpendicular fan-vaulting was probably by the architect of King's College Chapel, Cambridge, John Wastell. The vaulting above the choir and presbytery at **Oxford** cathedral (Christ Church) is an array of fan-vaulting, lierne vaulting, bosses and pendants. 'The most beautiful chapel in all Christendom', Henry VII's Chapel in Westminster Abbey, built in the early 1500s, takes the fan-vault to its climax. The very beautiful wooden roof above the nave at **St David's** cathedral was built at the end of the fifteenth century. Made of Irish oak it is a remarkable design of pendant arches, delicately carved.

We have already noted that there are numerous parish churches in the Perpendicular style. Some of these churches have since received cathedral status, notably **St Edmundsbury, Manchester,** and **Sheffield.** A church which owes much to the Perpendicular period is **Ripon** cathedral, sometimes called Ripon minster, which became a cathedral in 1836. It was partly transformed into a spacious Perpendicular church, but the fifteenth century builders failed to finish the work. This is especially noticeable at the crossing where the central tower possesses two round arches from the earlier church and two pointed ones where the transformation was begun—a unique feature.

When comparing the Norman nave arcade at **Gloucester** with the cathedral's Perpendicular choir and presbytery one realises that, architecturally speaking, we have come a very long way. Here indeed is an object lesson in the two contrasting styles. Regrettably there was no purpose-built cathedral exclusively in the Perpendicular style. Although Britain was becoming richer and more independent at this point in her history, more money was being directed towards undertakings other than cathedral churches.

Further Perpendicular features can be seen at: Bath Abbey (no longer a cathedral), Bradford, Chelmsford, Newcastle, St Albans, St Asaph, Wakefield and Worcester.

9. RUIN AND RENEWAL

From the Renaissance to the Gothic Revival

The sixteenth century was a time of religious and social upheaval which came fast in the wake of the Reformation. Following Henry VIII's break with Rome, monasteries were closed and many church treasures were commandeered by the Crown. It is not surprising that this period saw a general decline in church building and especially in cathedral building.

By the seventeenth century Old St. Paul's cathedral in London, one of the most splendid and largest of the Gothic cathedrals in Britain, was in an extremely ruinous condition. It was destroyed in the momentous Great Fire of London of 1666. The present St Paul's replacing it is the finest example of English Renaissance church architecture and as such it is unique among British cathedrals. Its designer, Sir Christopher Wren, adapted many Renaissance ideas he had learnt in Europe. A relative of his was bishop of Ely, and on his visits there the Octagon, the only Gothic dome, had no doubt made an impression on him. The term Renaissance perhaps needs an explanation. It means rebirth or revival and refers to the period in history when art was revitalised following the rediscovery of the ancient art of Rome and Greece.

St. Paul's cathedral, largely paid for by a tax on coal entering the Port of London, is built of Portland stone and took just under 35 years to complete. Sir Christopher Wren himself, although very old, was present to see the finish. Surmounting the famous dome, an unmistakable landmark, is the cross, 365 feet to its pinnacle. The entrance is approached by an impressive flight of steps to the portico. Inside we see huge round arches, Italian style, on massive square pillars leading to a vast central area with eight piers below the dome. The interior of St. Paul's is very ornate, enriched with panelling and mosaics, intricate carving by Grinling Gibbons and ironwork by Jean Tijou. A very poignant word *Resurgam* appears on a piece of stone above the south door in the south transept. It is said that Sir Christopher Wren came across it in the rubble of Old St. Pauls. It means *I shall rise again*. A new St. Paul's certainly has risen and withstood yet greater dangers in recent years, although it did sustain some war damage. Like many cathedrals it now faces enormous expense to prevent it from collapse.

The only part of the medieval parish church in **Derby,** (the church of All Saints, now a cathedral), that remained after demolition was the fine Perpendicular tower. The cathedral is one of the finest early eighteenth century churches in Britain. The architect was James Gibbs who also designed St. Martins-in-the-Fields in London, and this church is similar to it. In this century building has been necessary here to allow more space for the better conduct of cathedral worship around the high altar. The new design involves a partial rearrangement of the unique Bakewell screen—a superb piece of wrought-iron work by a local craftsman.

The Cathedral Church of St. Philip in **Birmingham** is in the English Baroque style. Built in the early 1700s, to the design of the famous Warwickshire architect Thomas Archer, this church is rectangular in shape. There is a gallery on each side of the nave with square fluted columns rising to a flat ceiling. The chancel is entered through a low wrought-iron screen, made perhaps by Jean Tijou. There are stained glass windows by Burne-Jones.

During the eighteenth century many of our great cathedrals were sadly neglected and allowed to fall into disrepair. This made restoration necessary in all of them to a greater or lesser degree. Already, in the mid-seventeenth century certain cathedrals had suffered extensive damage as a result of the Civil War. Stained glass was smashed. Statues were broken! Wood furnishings were burnt on soldiers' fires within the cathedrals themselves.Horses were stabled in the buildings as at **St Asaph.** After one battle hundreds of prisoners, captured by Oliver Cromwell, were marched to Durham and locked in the cathedral. The choir stalls and other wood furnishings were burned by the prisoners to keep warm.

Other cathedrals have unfortunately always been at a disadvantage as far as their stone work is concerned. Sandstone in particular does not stand up well to the elements, as cathedrals like **Lichfield** know only too well.

There were also restorers who, in the name of beauty, did much damage. James Wyatt was nicknamed 'the destroyer' after his work at **Salisbury,** where stained glass was removed 'because it made the cathedral dark'. Many restorers, however, rendered invaluable service and saved buildings from utter ruin. At **St Albans,** for example, Lord Grimthorpe financed extensive restoration, although the purist will maintain that Victorian additions and renovation here do not blend with the Norman and Gothic original. This is true in many places but we should nevertheless be grateful for the munificence and enthusiasm of such men even though it may have sometimes been misplaced. The Victorians were undoubtedly thorough, and their efforts were timely. **Lichfield** cathedral needed much restoration and nearly all the statues on the imposing West Front are Victorian replacements.

In the early 1800s a few parish churches in industrial areas were given cathedral status. **Manchester** and **Newcastle** are examples and both these churches have a long history. Unfortunately the beauty of the fine medieval church at Newcastle had faded during years of neglect so restoration there was considerable. This was the time of the Gothic Revival when design was inspired by the Middle Ages. **Blackburn** cathedral, with its tall pillars and pointed arches, is built in this style although it became a cathedral only fifty years or so ago. The present nave at **Bristol** was completed in 1888 since the plans to replace the Norman nave during the Middle Ages were never fulfilled. But despite the time lag the style of architecture is as it would have been. **Leicester** cathedral, considerably restored over the years, has a broach spire, rebuilt in the 1860s, unique for a cathedral.

The nave at **Southwark** was restored and completed in 1897. Over the years this church had been falling into ruin and the development of the railway at London Bridge threatened its very existence. There is Norman work and some exceptionally fine Gothic work, especially in the transepts, the choir, and the beautiful retro-choir beyond the high altar screen. Here on the south bank of the Thames this cathedral stands in a most unlikely but perhaps not unfortunate position. Though cramped by warehouses and thoroughfares, Southwark cathedral reminds us that the Church has an important part to play in a busy, modern world (plate 9).

10. THE TWENTIETH CENTURY

Truro cathedral is one of four Anglican ones built in Britain in the last hundred years. The style chosen by the architect, John Pearson, was Early English of the thirteenth century. The building, completed in 1910, is therefore very much 'out of period'. Part of the parish church of St. Mary (the rest was demolished) was incorporated into the new design, and the cathedral has interesting features and its three spires make an impressive skyline. (Pearson's son also carried out important extension work at **Wakefield** cathedral, a fine medieval church.)

Liverpool cathedral is also Gothic in conception with high soaring arches and a vault. Sir Giles Gilbert Scott, grandson of another famous architect, has not lived to see its completion. His prize-winning design was conceived in the early 1900s when he was 22 and it has of necessity been modified over the years. The lasting impression is one of vastness. However, a congregation several thousand strong can be seated so that each person has an uninterrupted view of the proceedings. This is partly due to the absence of pillars. The building is of local sand-stone and it will probably be completed in the 1970s. It will be the largest cathedral in Britain and among the five largest in the world.

Guildford and Liverpool are the only two Anglican Cathedrals built on new sites in this country since the Middle Ages. The central tower at **Guildford** is at the highest point of the hill. The design of the cathedral again follows the medieval pattern—with one vital difference. Unlike medieval worship, modern practice prefers an uninterrupted view of the high altar. There is therefore no screen across this church as was the pattern in old churches and, to quote the architect Sir Edward Maufe, R.A., 'the seven . . . simple . . . arches on each side lead us forward in spirit . . .'. The symbol of the cathedral is the Guildford Cross, the actual shape of the building, incorporating extra arms at the base, the welcoming arms of the Church symbolised by the unique west front.

In considering **Coventry** cathedral we have reached a building very much of the mid-twentieth century. It was designed by Sir Basil Spence. Lying north to south, the cathedral was completed in 1962 and covers the area north of the old cathedral destroyed in 1941. An impressive porch links the old ruins with the new building. Angels and saints are engraved on the huge 'west' window. From this point the eye is drawn to the high altar and, in place of the usual 'east' window, to the largest tapestry in the world, depicting Christ in Majesty. Designed by Graham Sutherland, it was actually woven in France. The Baptistry Window, a blaze of colour, is another memorable feature. The nave windows are set at an unusual angle so that their impact is only experienced to the full from the sanctuary. There is much symbolism in the various architectural features and furnishings. The Cross of Nails and the Charred Cross of Coventry in the ruined part are both poignant reminders of reconciliation, one of the main tasks facing the Christian Church today. Jacob Epstein's *St Michael and Satan* is just outside the entrance (plate 8).

At **Llandaff** there has been a similar 'resurrection' after the land-mine damage of 1941. We can still see much of the original building but the most outstanding modern feature is Jacob Epstein's *Majestas* in unpolished aluminium, on a concrete arch-cum-pulpitum. The latter was conceived by the architect to allow an uninterrupted view the length of the cathedral, but at the same time also allowing the traditional break between nave and choir (plate 12).

Modern extension work has been carried out at Derby, Portsmouth, Sheffield and St. Edmundsbury cathedrals. Old and new have been fused together in many cathedrals and **Portsmouth** cathedral is no exception. Parts of the building remind us of the church's distant origins in late Norman and early Gothic times. In the seventeenth century the tower and nave, damaged in the Civil War, were rebuilt by order of Charles II. Now this ancient church is being refashioned in keeping with its new cathedral status.

In the past twenty years or so work has gone on to enlarge the cathedral church of St Peter and St Paul at **Sheffield.** The new section here is very extensive—almost a completely new church. Work has been carried out on the nave, St. George's Chapel, a further tower and a narthax—a kind of porch, and a chapel to the Holy Spirit beyond the high altar.

1970, the 1100th anniversary of the martyrdom of King Edmund of East Anglia, saw the consecration of the new eastward extension of **St Edmundsbury** cathedral. Of the great Abbey of St. Edmund there are only a few impressive ruins, relics of the great monastic centre whose church was once reckoned to be the third largest in Christendom. The cathedral today is also the parish church of St James, originally built, together with two other churches, for the townsfolk to worship in away from the monks. This is no doubt one reason why the abbey itself did not become the parish church as it did elsewhere, at St Albans for example. The tall slender pillars of the nave at St Edmundsbury make it a particularly fine example of the work of John Wastell who lived in Bury St Edmunds until his death in 1515. The current rebuilding and extension here are part of an ambitious plan to make this church even more worthy of its twentieth century function as the mother church of the Diocese of Suffolk.

11. GLASS, STONE AND WOOD

There are three visual arts which particularly come into their own in a cathedral. They are stained glass, and stone and wood carving. Indeed it was the Church, and in particular the great cathedrals and abbeys, which were among the earliest patrons of these arts.

The man in charge of the actual building of a medieval cathedral was the master mason. He was responsible for drawing up plans, choosing stone at the quarry and employing labourers and craftsmen—the stone-masons, the carpenters, the glaziers, the stone-carvers and so on. Each mason identified the stone on which he had been working with his own mason's mark. This helped when his wages were being calculated and also encouraged a high standard of workmanship. Some very skilled craftsmen were much in demand and they travelled from one place to another. The craftsmen also had their own guilds, not unlike our trade unions, and they lived on the building-site in lean-to huts called lodges. Once the building of a particular part of a cathedral was completed many craftsmen could start work on the pillars, the roof and the window spaces.

Stained glass

The glaziers had their own craft guilds of which there were over fifty in York alone. Five to six hundred years ago the making of stained glass, although expensive, was far more widespread than it is today. Colourful windows to beautify the churches and tell the story of Christianity to illiterate people were thought a necessity for the House of God, more so even than a good floor! One of the most important centres for making stained glass was in York. Some of the windows in the Minster today were made in workshops in Stonegate. One method of producing stained glass was to add colour to molten glass. Another way was to brush paint over small fragments and then scratch the design on to them. After reheating the glass to fix the design the pieces were joined together with lead, very much like a glass jig-saw puzzle! All this was then carefully raised into the window space where more lead fittings were prepared in the stone supports and transoms.

York Minster possesses the oldest fragment of stained glass in the country, dated *c*. 1150. Also in the Minster is the famous window called The Five Sisters, now over 700 years old. Unlike most stained glass, which is pictorial, the glass in these five lancet windows is covered with abstract patterns in yellows, greens and browns with a greeny-grey background, which is called grisaille. This type of glass is especially translucent and these are the finest examples in the country. Throughout the Minster there are many fine examples of stained glass. They represent more than half of all the precious stained glass in the City of York and this city has more than any other in the whole of Britain. The huge east window was made by the glass painter John Thornton of Coventry at the beginning of the fifteenth century.

Dating from about 1350, the great east window at **Gloucester** is the largest of its kind in Britain and it contains much of its original glass. It is, in a sense, a war memorial to those involved in the French wars of the fourteenth century. Known as the Crecy window, it was built soon after that battle. It embodies two side pieces at an angle, enabling the use of as much glass as possible.

At **Canterbury** are the Miracle Windows, made about 1200. Soon after the murder of Becket some monks wrote a record of the miracles which had taken place at the martyr's tomb. These were translated into stained glass and set up in the windows around the shrine.

At **Lincoln,** the Dean's Eye is a great rose window in the north transept also dating from the beginning of the thirteenth century. Across in the south transept is the Bishop's Eye.

Stone carving

Of examples of stone carving, the famous Leaves of **Southwell** have already been mentioned—a delightful array of foliage which includes ivy, hawthorn, hop, oak and many others, with pigs, lizards, birds and dogs. Of a much earlier date there are Romanesque carvings at **Rochester, Ely** and **Lincoln** and in the crypt at **Canterbury. Chichester** possesses two of the earliest and most famous sculptures depicting Christ. At **Wells** the capitals of the pillars in the nave and transepts are of the famous stiff-leaf design, unique to England. Some of the carvings tell a story; for example, of the fruit stealers and their downfall! Amidst the leaves appear birds, strange creatures and grotesque heads.

Wood carving

Many cathedrals, notably **Chester** (plate 19), **Manchester** and **Ripon,** possess some very fine wood carving. Misericords or misereri seats are wonderfully carved on the undersides. These are a form of tip-up seat with a small carved projection, against which the priest or monk could lean for support when standing during the very lengthy services. The subjects of the carvings are of great variety. Among the **Norwich** misericords there is a schoolmaster whacking a naughty boy; at **Worcester** the seasons are represented; **Manchester** choir stalls include a fox featured in various situations; at **Ripon** various biblical stories are depicted—Joshua and Caleb carrying grapes, and Jonah and the whale. The **Winchester** cathedral choir stalls are among the earliest. These even include a carved face with a moving tongue! At **Chester** the desk ends are also extremely fine, depicting a Jesse tree, an elephant and castle (also at **Ripon**) and a delightful little chap with his walking stick. The craftsmen were obviously not limited to what we would acknowledge as 'sacred' subjects, and must have enjoyed themselves, poking fun at their contemporaries, for the carvings are often full of symbolism.

Exeter has a superb bishop's throne, sixty feet high and most exquisitely carved in the early 1300s. **St. Paul's** cathedral has superb carving by the Renaissance craftsman Grinling Gibbons. At **Durham,** where the stalls were burned for firewood by prisoners in the seventeenth century, these stalls were replaced, but the name of the craftsman is not known.

The Western Towers of Durham Cathedral and (right) the massive Central Tower of York Minster.

G. N. Wright

1. *Salisbury Cathedral has the loftiest spire in Britain and is a unique example of a complete Early English cathedral.*

Iris Hardwick

2. *Exeter Cathedral is the finest example of Decorated Gothic architecture in England.*

3. *The fourteenth-century Octagon at Ely Cathedral. The rest of the building is mostly Norman.*

J. W. Whitelaw

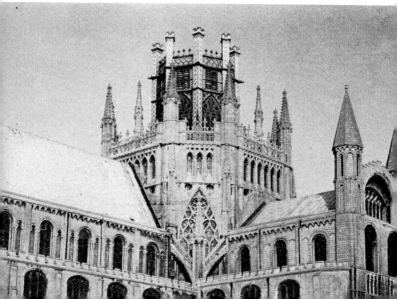

G. N. Wright

4. *St David's Cathedral in Dyfed was probably founded early in the sixth century.*

5. *St Albans Abbey is both a cathedral and a parish church.*

C. Lamb

J. W. Whitelaw

6. Norwich Cathedral has a fine Norman nave and intricately carved ceiling bosses.

J. W. Whitelaw

7. *The three spires of Lichfield Cathedral are known as the Ladies of the Vale.*

9. Southwark Cathedral, somewhat cramped by warehouses on London's south bank, has a beautiful Gothic retro choir and many interesting associations.

C. Lamb

G. H. Haines

8. Jacob Epstein's 'St Michael and Satan' at Coventry Cathedral is one of many modern works of art incorporated into the building.

10. Canterbury Cathedral has much of the finest twelfth-century stained glass in Britain. This is Adam, from the west window of the nave.

G. H. Haines

11. *Worcester Cathedral has the earliest Perpendicular central tower. Charles II is said to have watched the battle of Worcester from it.*

J. A. Long

12. *Llandaff Cathedral has its nave dominated by Jacob Epstein's sculpture 'Majestas'.*

E. Preston

13. *Hereford Cathedral is renowned for its chained library
and 'Mappa Mundi', a map of the world drawn in 1290.*

D. Uttley

14. *The unique 'scissor' arches at Wells Cathedral.*

D. Uttley

15. Gloucester Cathedral's nave has Norman pillars. The cathedral was originally a Benedictine abbey.

J. W. Whitelaw

16. *Peterborough Cathedral has one of the most impressive
west fronts, with tall recessed arches.*

17. The vault of the Guardian Angel's Chapel at Winchester Cathedral is decorated with mid thirteenth-century wall paintings.

18. The detached bell-tower at Chichester Cathedral is a rare feature in England.

E. Preston

19. Chester Cathedral is noted for the fine medieval wood
carving in the choir-stalls.

12. CATHEDRALS OF ENGLAND AND WALES

Note: Cathedral plans are not to scale.

BANGOR, Cathedral Church of St Deiniol
Cathedral of ancient origin, the oldest in Britain.
Diocese: Practically the modern county of Gwynedd.
Note especially: Small size. Cruciform shape. 15th century font. Towers. The Bound Rood. The Mostyn Christ. Tomb of Welsh Prince, Owain Gwynedd (died 1170). Floor tiles. Mural by Brian Thomas.

A monastery was founded here in 525 by St Deiniol who became bishop in 546 and this church was his cathedral. The fabric has suffered from invaders and native rebels and has undergone frequent repair. There are few remains of the Norman church; most of the present fabric is of 16th century; last restoration was in 1960s.

BIRMINGHAM, Cathedral Church of St Philip
Became a cathedral in 1905.
Diocese: Birmingham, Aston, parts of south Staffordshire, parts of north Worcestershire, other parts of Warwickshire.
Note especially: Galleries above side aisles. Rectangular shape with eastern part added. Wrought-iron screen. Stained glass by Burne-Jones. Belfry tower. Memorial to Bishop Wilson, 'Confessor for the Faith' as a prisoner of war.

King George I gave £600 towards cost of completing this church, built in early 1700s to the design of the famous Warwickshire architect Thomas Archer. Product of 'Protestant' Christianity. Like St Paul's London, a post-reformation cathedral. Emphasis on preaching in layout of such churches.

BLACKBURN, Cathedral Church of St Mary the Virgin
Became a cathedral in 1926.
Diocese: An area within Lancashire.
Note especially: Western tower. Octagonal tower at the crossing. Blending of new and old. Modern figure sculpture of Christ the Worker. Replica of 15th century Pax of Madonna and Child.

The Nave is in the Gothic style of the late Middle Ages, built in the early 1800s, the years of the Gothic Revival.

BRADFORD, Cathedral Church of St Peter
Became a cathedral in 1919.
Diocese: Parts of the West Riding of Yorkshire, small parts of Westmorland and Lancashire.
Note especially: The tower, nearly 100 feet high. Coloured

roof bosses and angels. Mason's marks. The Flaxman sculpture. The new extension.

St Blaise, the patron saint of the city and of wool-combers, is featured above the Provost's stall. In Civil War sieges of 17th century wool-packs protected the exterior of the tower from cannon balls. Much destruction throughout history. Rebuilt in Perpendicular style in 15th century.

BRECON, Cathedral Church of St John the Evangelist
Became a cathedral in 1923.

Diocese: This is called Swansea and Brecon. Covers Brecknockshire, Radnorshire, Swansea, east and west Gower in Glamorganshire.

Note especially: Early English chancel and east window. Lancets. Norman font. Early type of lighting—the cresset stone with cups. The Havard Chapel.

The first Norman lord here founded this priory in the same way as Duke William had founded a monastery at Battle, scene of the battle of Hastings. There was once a rood-screen, venerated by pilgrims.

BRISTOL, Cathedral Church of the Holy and Undivided Trinity
Became a cathedral in 1542.

Diocese: City of Bristol, parts of Gloucestershire and Wiltshire.

Note especially: Internal buttresses. Star-shaped recesses. Norman vestibule and chapter house. Elder Lady Chapel and Lady Chapel.

A 'hall church', unique in England. Augustinian monastery founded here in 12th century. Traditional site of famous oak tree where Augustine met other Christians. Nave built in last century in medieval style.

CANTERBURY, Cathedral Church of Christ
Founded as a cathedral in 597. The 'Mother' church of the Anglican Communion.

Diocese: Whole of east Kent, east of River Medway and rural Deanery of Croydon.

Note especially: All of it! Stained glass (plate 10). Perpendicular nave. Central tower—The Bell Harry. Site of Archbishop Thomas Becket's Martyrdom (1170). St Augustine's Chair. Pilgrim steps. Crypt.

People: 101 archbishops including Augustine and Thomas Becket. Edward the Black Prince. King Henry IV. Geoffrey Chaucer—*The Canterbury Tales.*

Monastery and cathedral established by mission from Rome in 597. Various stages of building. Becket's shrine became one of the most visited ones in Christendom in the Middle Ages. Pilgrims travelled the Pilgrims' Way between Winchester and Canterbury and from London, like Chaucer. Considerable restoration, especially of priceless glass.

CANTERBURY CATHEDRAL

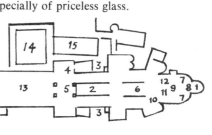

1   Corona
2   Choir
3   Norman towers
4   The Martyrdom
5   Central tower
6   High Altar
7   Miracle glass
8   St Augustine's chair
9   Site of shrine
10 Pilgrim steps
11 Tomb of Black Prince
12 Tomb of Henry IV

13 Nave
14 Cloisters
15 Chapter house

CARLISLE, Cathedral Church of the Holy and Undivided Trinity

Became a cathedral in 1133.

Diocese: Most of Cumberland, most of Westmorland and a small part of Lancashire.

Note especially: Great east window. Choir stall paintings. Screens. Misericords. Carved capitals on choir pillars. Norman nave much shortened.

People: St Kentigern. Augustinian monks. Robert Bruce. Edward I. Sir Walter Scott married Miss Carpenter here.

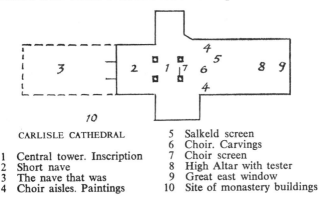

CARLISLE CATHEDRAL

1   Central tower. Inscription
2   Short nave
3   The nave that was
4   Choir aisles. Paintings
5   Salkeld screen
6   Choir. Carvings
7   Choir screen
8   High Altar with tester
9   Great east window
10 Site of monastery buildings

51

History has not been kind to this cathedral. Vandalism from Civil War soldiers. Tragic fires earlier. Inscription *Deo Gracias* 'Thanks be to God' set into the floor symbolises thanksgiving for God's blessing through troubled history.

CHELMSFORD, Cathedral Church of St Mary the Virgin, St Peter and St Cedd

Became a cathedral in 1914.

Diocese: All of Essex, parts of Suffolk and a small part of Kent.

Note especially: Carvings on the outside of the tower. South porch. East Anglian chequered flint work on exterior walls. Double arch in chancel.

People: Probably St Cedd, evangelist of East Saxons. Maurice, Bishop of London held manor and in 1100 bridged the rivers Can and Chelmer.

St Peter, depicted as a modern fisherman, is the subject of a statue on the exterior of south chapel. Links with Saxon cathedral of St Peter at Bradwell-on-sea, founded by St Cedd over 1300 years ago.

CHESTER, Cathedral Church of Christ and The Blessed Virgin Mary

Became a cathedral in 1541.

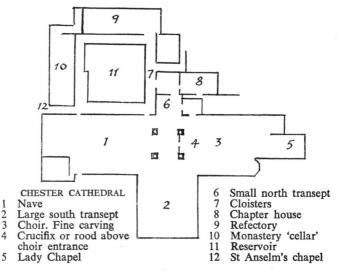

CHESTER CATHEDRAL

1 Nave
2 Large south transept
3 Choir. Fine carving
4 Crucifix or rood above choir entrance
5 Lady Chapel
6 Small north transept
7 Cloisters
8 Chapter house
9 Refectory
10 Monastery 'cellar'
11 Reservoir
12 St Anselm's chapel

Diocese: Cheshire (The County Palatine of Chester).

Note especially: Monastic buildings. Refectory pulpit. Medieval woodcarving in the choir-stalls (plate 19). Different sizes of transepts.

People: St Werburgh, an Anglo-Saxon princess. St Anselm from Bec in Normandy (an Archbishop of Canterbury). Benedictine monks, some of whom wrote the famous *Chester Miracle Plays* performed by trade guilds. Charles I.

Shrine of St Werburgh was focal point for pilgrimage in Middle Ages. Normans established Benedictine monastery. Much rebuilding and extension of the church from 13th century onwards. South transept once a separate parish church until 100 years ago.

CHICHESTER, Cathedral Church of the Holy Trinity

Became a cathedral in 1070 (Selsey 681).

Diocese: All of Sussex.

Note especially: Various styles from Norman to Perpendicular. Early stone sculpture. Detached bell-tower (rare in

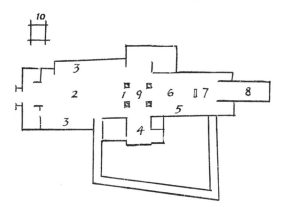

CHICHESTER CATHEDRAL	
1 Screen	5 Romanesque sculptures
2 Wide nave	6 Choir
3 Chapels adding to nave width	7 Retro choir. Site of shrine
4 South transept. Window	8 Lady Chapel
	9 Central tower. Spire
	10 Detached bell-tower

England). Bell-Arundel screen. Modern furnishings including tapestry and pulpit.

People: St Wilfrid (also very much linked with Ripon). St Richard of Chichester, died 1253. As bishop he won the hearts of his people. His shrine here was a great place of pilgrimage.

A surprisingly wide nave but, for a Norman cathedral, seems of modest size. In the retro-choir behind the High Altar the best parts of the cathedral are to be seen, dating from about 1199, after the fire of 1157. The central tower spire collapsed in 1861 and was later cleverly rebuilt.

COVENTRY, Cathedral Church of St Michael

Refounded as a cathedral in 1918. New cathedral 1962 (Old St Michael's destroyed 1940).

Diocese: Part of Warwickshire except Birmingham.

Note especially: All of it! Contemporary furnishings. Graham Sutherland tapestry. Stained glass windows. The Baptistry window designed by John Piper. Epstein's 'St Michael and Satan' (plate 8). Chapel of Unity and Chapel of Christ the Servant.

People: Lady Godiva benefactor of neighbouring Benedictine monastery. Medieval trade guilds with their miracle/mystery plays revived in recent years.

In vision of purpose this cathedral is making a break with tradition. Designed by Sir Basil Spence, it is traditional in layout although the architecture is of our times employing modern materials and techniques. There is much symbolism in the modern furnishings and architectural features. Old and new, death and resurrection, forgiveness, reconciliation.

DERBY, Cathedral Church of All Saints

Became a cathedral in 1927.

Diocese: Derbyshire.

Note especially: Western tower, almost 180 feet high. Wrought-iron screen. Various monuments, especially that to 'Bess of Hardwick', Countess of Shrewsbury. Altar and baldacchino. Modern coloured glass.

In 1723 the vicar of the original church here, assisted by a gang of hired labourers, is said to have pulled the church to pieces in one night, since it was already in a ruinous state. Rebuilding followed in the Renaissance style although the fine perpendicular styled western tower remained. The architect was James Gibbs. There are modern extensions to a sympathetic design by Sebastian Comper who adapted his distinguished father's plans.

DURHAM, Cathedral Church of Christ and Blessed Mary the Virgin

Founded as a cathedral about 997 (Diocese 635).

Diocese: County Durham.

Note especially: All of it! Impressive site. Finest Norman Romanesque, especially nave pillars. Earliest rib vaulting in Europe. Bronze sanctuary door knocker.

People: St Cuthbert of Lindisfarne (Holy Island). The Venerable Bede. Annual University and Miners' services.

Built for the tomb of St Cuthbert who died in 687 on a lonely Farne island. His body was carried from place to place for years during Viking invasions. This fine peninsula formed by the river Wear provided a final place of refuge for the monks. A simple grey slab marks his burial place behind the High Altar, an important place of pilgrimage for hundreds of years right up to the present. The Venerable Bede, a scholarly monk from Jarrow, the Father of English History, is buried in the unique Galilee Chapel. In all its massiveness, Durham has been called 'the Norman Lord' as opposed to Ely in the south, 'the Norman Lady'.

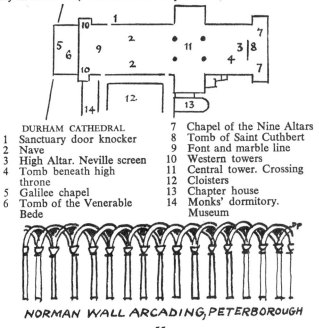

DURHAM CATHEDRAL

1 Sanctuary door knocker
2 Nave
3 High Altar. Neville screen
4 Tomb beneath high throne
5 Galilee chapel
6 Tomb of the Venerable Bede
7 Chapel of the Nine Altars
8 Tomb of Saint Cuthbert
9 Font and marble line
10 Western towers
11 Central tower. Crossing
12 Cloisters
13 Chapter house
14 Monks' dormitory. Museum

NORMAN WALL ARCADING, PETERBOROUGH

ELY, Cathedral Church of the Holy and Undivided Trinity and St Etheldreda

Became a cathedral in 1109.

Diocese: Cambridgeshire, Isle of Ely, parts of Huntingdonshire and Norfolk.

Note especially: All of it! Impressive view from the Fens. Norman nave. The Octagon—the only Gothic dome (plate 3). The Lady Chapel. Sculptured corbels of events in St Etheldreda's life.

People: St Etheldreda, the first Abbess of the monastery for monks and nuns here, 1300 years ago. Her shrine later stood near the eastern end. Hereward the Wake made his famous stand against the Normans here. Oliver Cromwell lived locally. He banned services for ten years.

Basically Norman. Great length. Later additions. Very notable work in 14th century on the amazing Octagon designed by the monk-architect Alan of Walsingham. This great fenland church is 'the Norman Lady'. In the half light it has also been described as a ship on an ocean.

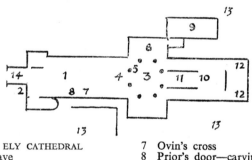

	ELY CATHEDRAL	7	Ovin's cross
1	Nave	8	Prior's door—carving
2	West front	9	Lady Chapel
3	Octagon and lantern	10	Site of shrine
4	Tomb of Alan of Walsingham	11	Choir
5	Sculptures	12	Chantry chapels
6	North transept. Wooden roof	13	Monastery buildings and ruins
		14	Galilee porch

EXETER, Cathedral Church of St Peter

Became a cathedral about 1050 (Crediton 909).

Diocese: Almost the whole of Devon, one parish in Somerset.

Note especially: All of it! Finest Decorated Gothic in England (plate 2). 'Palm' vaulting. Carvings in wood and stone. Earliest misericords. Choir screen. Captain Scott's flag. Minstrels' gallery. Acrobat carving. The Cathedra.

People: St Boniface was educated in the monastery. King Canute was a benefactor.

Most cathedrals present a patchwork of styles. This is one of the few that does not. A building of remarkable symmetry. Unique also in that there is no central tower but two side towers above the transepts. Suffered damage from air raid in 1942.

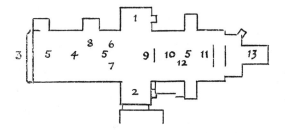

	EXETER CATHEDRAL	7	Madonna corbel
1	North transept tower	8	Minstrels' gallery
2	South transept tower	9	Screen or pulpitum
3	West front. Window	10	Choir
4	Nave	11	High Altar. East window
5	Continuous vaulted ceiling	12	Bishop's throne
6	Tumbler corbel	13	Lady Chapel

GLOUCESTER, Cathedral Church of the Holy and Indivisible Trinity

Became a cathedral in 1541.

Diocese: Much of Gloucestershire, parts of Wiltshire, Oxfordshire, Worcestershire, Herefordshire and Warwickshire.

Note especially: All of it! Norman nave pillars (plate 15). Perpendicular choir and presbytery. East window (largest). Earliest fan vaulting in cloisters. Monks' lavatorium. Korean prisoner-of-war cross.

People: William the Conqueror is said to have commissioned the Domesday Book here. His eldest son Robert is buried here. The murdered king Edward II is buried here. He was venerated as a martyr king and there is a fine alabaster effigy of him. His tomb attracted pilgrims

The Benedictine monastery was founded in 681. Then came Norman building. Unique perpendicular east end.

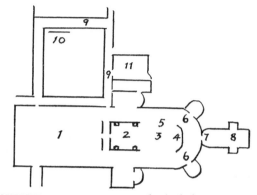

GLOUCESTER CATHEDRAL

1 Nave
2 Choir. Central tower
3 Tomb of Robert, son of William I
4 Great east window
5 Tomb of Edward II

6 Ambulatory
7 Lady Chapel 'bridge'
8 Lady Chapel
9 Cloisters. Early fan vaulting
10 Lavatorium—monks' washing place
11 Chapter house

GUILDFORD, Cathedral Church of the Holy Spirit
The new diocese was formed in 1927.

Diocese: West Surrey and parts of north Hampshire.

Note especially: West Front. Engravings on glass. Embroidered kneelers. Modern furnishings. Sanctuary carpet. Brass stag marking summit of hill.

Guildford and Liverpool cathedrals are the only two Anglican ones built on new sites in this country since the Middle Ages. The wooden cross was erected on the site in 1933. Certain bricks in the building are made of the very clay of Stag Hill itself. The foundation stone was laid in 1936. War interrupted progress. The consecration was in 1961. Designed by Sir Edward Maufe.

HEREFORD, Cathedral Church of the Blessed Virgin Mary and St Ethelbert
Founded as a cathedral in 676.

Diocese: Herefordshire, parts of Worcestershire, Shropshire. Radnorshire and Montgomeryshire.

Note especially: Various styles, especially late Norman and Early English. Central tower. Chained library. The Map of the World, *Mappa Mundi* (1290). Vicars' cloister. Old wooden pulpit. Very ancient chair.

People: St Ethelbert (a king of East Anglia) martyred near here in Saxon times. St Thomas Cantelupe, Lord High Treasurer of England, appointed bishop in 1275. Both shrines were visited by countless pilgrims. Nell Gwynn was born in a cottage near the cathedral.

Hereford, and not least its cathedral, one of the smallest and oldest, was often ravaged by war since it is situated in the Welsh border country—the Welsh Marches. Together with Gloucester and Worcester, Hereford cathedral is associated with the annual Three Choirs Festival, the oldest musical festival in Europe.

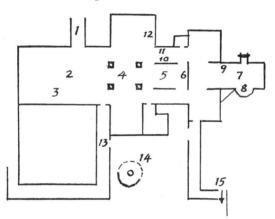

HEREFORD CATHEDRAL		8	Bishop Audley's chantry
		9	Entrance to crypt
1	North or Booth porch	10	Map of the World—
2	Nave		Mappa Mundi
3	Ancient pulpit	11	Entrance to chained library
4	Central tower	12	Shrine of Bishop Cantilupe
5	Choir	13	Bishop's cloister
6	High Altar. Norman arch	14	Ruin of chapter house
7	Lady Chapel	15	Vicars' cloister

LEICESTER, Cathedral Church of St Martin

Became a cathedral in 1927 (the Diocese is very ancient).
Diocese: Leicestershire.
Note especially: Broach spire. Chancel arch. Choir gallery

at west end. Stained glass window of St Martin and the beggar. Timber roofs.

A fine town church, probably on the site of a Roman temple and later a Saxon church. Basically this church was built in the 13th, 14th and 15th centuries. Considerable restoration and refurnishing has taken place in the last hundred years or so.

LICHFIELD, Cathedral Church of the Blessed Virgin Mary and St Chad

Original cathedral foundation was about 700 (Mercia 656).

Diocese: Most of Staffordshire, parts of Shropshire and Warwickshire.

Note especially: The three spires (plate 7). Chapel of St Chad's Head. Arcading in chapter house vestibule. Chapter house. Gospel manuscripts. Cheshire cat carving. The Sleeping Children monument.

People: St Chad died in 672 and was buried here in the first Mercian cathedral. In 1195 a new cathedral was built for his shrine, much visited by pilgrims. Bishop Selwyn was first bishop of New Zealand before he came to Lichfield 1868. Also commemorated is Dr Samuel Johnson of literary fame, a man of Lichfield.

Lichfield was an important Christian centre in Saxon times. The kingdom of Mercia covered the Midlands, and Lichfield was at one time the headquarters of an archbishop. The cathedral suffered badly at the hands of Civil War extremists in the 17th century. A further disadvantage is the rather poor quality of the dark red sandstone which, as in other places also, has not weathered well. Considerable renovation has always been necessary.

LINCOLN, Cathedral Church of the Blessed Virgin Mary

Founded as a cathedral about 1072 (Dorchester 886, Leicester 680, Lindine 678).

Diocese: Lincolnshire.

Note especially: All of it! Three great towers. Angel Choir and Lincoln Imp. Choir stalls. Double arcading against walls. Stained glass. 'Trondheim' pillar. South-east porch. Impressive site. Copy of Magna Carta.

People: St Hugh buried in the Angel Choir. He came from Avalon in France towards the end of 12th century. His shrine became a focal point for pilgrims. There were no monks here. This was a minster, served by mission priests who travelled the district evangelising.

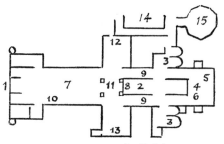

	LINCOLN CATHEDRAL		
1	West front. Towers	8	Pulpitum
2	Choir	9	Choir aisles
3	Eastern transepts	10	Tournai marble font
4	Angel choir	11	Central tower. Crossing
5	Lincoln Imp carving	12	Dean's Eye window
6	Line of 'chevet'	13	Bishop's Eye window
7	**Nave**	14	Cloisters
		15	Chapter house

LIVERPOOL, Cathedral Church of Christ

Diocese formed 1880, foundation stone 1904.
Diocese: West Derby hundred of Lancashire except for the part in the diocese of Manchester. Wigan.
Note especially: Massive tower. Vastness throughout the building. Early 20th century furnishings.

The 'Cathedral of the Seaport'—such is the apt description, coined some years ago, for this vast building built north to south, parallel to the river Mersey. Of local sandstone, it will be completed probably during the 1970s, and it will then be among the five largest cathedrals in the world and the largest in Britain.

LLANDAFF, Cathedral Church of St Peter and St Paul

Original foundation: Mid 6th century.
Diocese: Most of Glamorganshire.
Note especially: Modern renovation. Epstein sculpture *Majestas* (plate 12). St David's Chapel. 19th century porcelain panels. Celtic cross. Gargoyles. Unusual three-faced carving in nave.
People: Teilo, a 6th century monk worked as a missionary here. His *llan* or church was sited near the river Taff, hence

61

the name Llan(t)daff. His tomb is near the High Altar.

In Middle Ages the church grew in size and beauty. The 17th and 18th centuries brought neglect and ruin. Almost complete destruction came by a land-mine in 1941. Among British cathedrals, next to Coventry, Llandaff endured the greatest war damage. There has not been an entirely new building here but the core of the original church has become part of the new creation.

LONDON (ST PAUL'S), Cathedral Church of St Paul

Founded as a cathedral in 604 (Diocese 314).

Diocese: City of London, Westminster, former Middlesex, boroughs of County of London north of the Thames.

Note especially: All of it! Fine Renaissance architecture. The dome and Whispering Gallery. Tombs of great national figures. The crypt.

People: Sir Christopher Wren the architect. His craftsmen include Jean Tijou (ironwork) and Grinling Gibbons (wood-carving). Dr John Donne (1621-31 Dean of Old St Paul's)— his monument is the only item to survive the Great Fire of 1666.

A truly 'national shrine' replacing one of the largest medieval cathedrals.

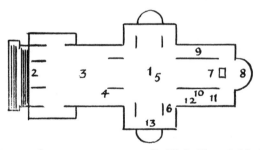

ST PAUL'S CATHEDRAL

1 Dome. Whispering Gallery
2 West front. Portico
3 Nave
4 Painting 'The Light of the World'
5 Nelson's tomb, below in crypt
6 Entrance to crypt and OBE Chapel
7 High Altar. Baldachino
8 American Memorial Chapel
9 North choir aisle Tijou screen
10 South choir aisle Tijou screen
11 Lady Chapel
12 Dr John Donne effigy
13 South door 'Resurgam' inscription

MANCHESTER, Cathedral and Collegiate Church of St Mary, St Denys and St George

Became a cathedral in 1847.

Diocese: Parts of Lancashire. Manchester and Rochdale archdeaconries.

Note especially: Wooden ceiling. Choir-stall carvings. The rood screen. Saxon stone.

In spite of its 130 foot tower some people are unaware of this cathedral. A concentration of commercial buildings and such like associated with a great city like Manchester can overshadow even a cathedral! Its long history goes back to Saxon times but the present building is very much a product of the late Middle Ages and of recent restoration.

NEWCASTLE, Cathedral Church of St Nicholas

Became a cathedral in 1882.

Diocese: City of Newcastle, Northumberland, parts of Cumberland.

Note especially: West tower and 'crown' lantern. Fine octagonal font and canopy. A few pre-reformation features.

A little church was built on this site in the centre of the city soon after the arrival of the Normans. There was re-building later. The 16th and 17th centuries were times of great unrest. John Knox, the Scottish Reformer, preached here.

NEWPORT, Cathedral Church of St Woolos

Became a cathedral officially in 1949.

Diocese: Called the Diocese of Monmouth, created in 1921.

Note especially: West tower. Norman arches. Carvings on the capitals. Modern extension.

Legend says that, in the 6th century, Gwynllyw, or Woolos, was converted to Christianity. Here on Stow Hill, in obedience to a vision, he had a little church built to commemorate his conversion. The present St Mary's Chapel is most likely the site of his church.

NORWICH, Cathedral Church of the Holy and Undivided Trinity

Built as a cathedral about 1096 (Thetford 1070; Dunwich 630, North Elmham 673).

Diocese: Most of Norfolk, small part of Suffolk.

Note especially: All of it! Norman work in nave and apse (plate 6). Late Gothic work. Ceiling bosses. Unique bishop's throne. Central tower and spire. Cloisters.

People: Benedictine monks. Norwich painters in the Middle Ages produced beautiful work, examples of which can be seen in the cathedral. The grave of Nurse Cavell is near the eastern end outside the cathedral.

Norwich had its fair share of setbacks and disturbance in the Middle Ages. Although basically a Norman building, the ceilings throughout are later additions. A short distance east of the cathedral is the famous Pull's Ferry water gate through which passed a canal linking the close with the river Wensum.

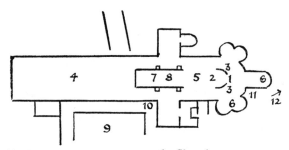

NORWICH CATHEDRAL

1 Bishop's throne in apse
2 High Altar
3 Apse and ambulatory
4 Nave
5 Presbytery

6 Chapel
7 Choir
8 Central tower. Spire
9 Cloisters
10 Prior's door
11 Nurse Cavell's tomb
12 To Pull's Ferry water-gate

OXFORD, Cathedral Church of Christ

Became a cathedral in 1545 (Diocese 1542).

Diocese: One of the largest, over 2,200 sq. miles. Oxfordshire, Berkshire and Buckinghamshire.

Note especially: 'Double' Norman arches. Fine vaulted ceiling above choir. St Frideswide's shrine. Jacobean woodwork.

People: St Frideswide, a Saxon lady of noble birth. Her name means 'bond of peace'. She founded a church here 1200 years ago. The scholars of the Oxford Movement which was centred on this city in the last century, helped so much to revitalise the Church of England.

One never hears of 'Oxford Cathedral'. However, Christ Church, as it is familiarly known, is the only College Chapel that is also a cathedral. Of modest size and of somewhat unusual shape, if it were not for the 13th century spire, one of the earliest, few people would know of the cathedral's whereabouts, amidst all the college buildings.

PETERBOROUGH, Cathedral Church of St Peter, St Paul and St Andrew

Became a cathedral in 1541.

Diocese: Northamptonshire and Rutland.

Note especially: All of it! Norman architecture almost throughout. Apse. Wooden nave ceiling. Perpendicular 'New Building'. Burial places of two queens. West front arches (plate 16).

People: A sacred relic, the arm of King Oswald of Northumbria who was killed in battle in 642, was one of several relics collected by the monks here. Hereward the Wake, in an effort to drive out the Normans, set the monastery on fire. Queen Catherine of Aragon, first wife of King Henry VIII, was buried here after her death at Kimbolton, not far away. Mary, Queen of Scots, was beheaded at Fotheringhay Castle and also buried here originally. The gravedigger, Robert Scarlett, lived to the age of 98.

A great Fenland abbey, a stronghold of the Church since the 7th century, Peterborough Cathedral has not always received the 'tourist' attention it deserves.

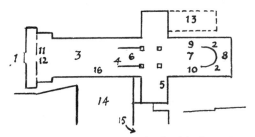

PETERBOROUGH CATHEDRAL	
1 West front	9 Burial place of Catherine of Aragon
2 Apse	10 First burial place of Mary, Queen of Scots
3 Nave. Wooden ceiling	11 Robert Scarlett's portrait
4 King Oswald carving	12 West door. Carving at base
5 St Oswald's Chapel	13 Site of Lady Chapel
6 Choir	14 Cloister
7 Presbytery	15 Monastic ruins
8 New 'Perpendicular' building	

PORTSMOUTH, Cathedral Church of St Thomas of Canterbury

Became a cathedral in 1927.

Diocese: Parts of Hampshire, the Isle of Wight.

Note especially: Various associations with the sea. Relics of the *Victory*. The Navy Aisle. Plaque of the Madonna and Child (1500). Stone Gallery beneath the tower—the Jube. Illuminated service books. North wall stones. Overseas stones. D-Day stone.

Old and new are fused together here but the work of extension is not complete. Throughout its long history the tower and its predecessor have served as watch tower, signalling base and lighthouse.

RIPON, Cathedral Church of St Peter and St Wilfrid

Became a cathedral in 1836 (also for a brief period in Saxon times).

Diocese: Parts of the West and North Ridings of Yorkshire.

Note especially: Saxon crypt (unique). Transitional-Norman and Gothic architecture. Unusual tower arches. East window. Misericords.

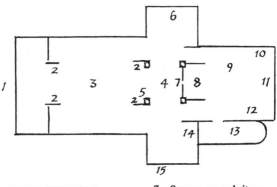

RIPON CATHEDRAL

1 West front
2 Evidence of earlier church
3 Wide nave
4 Central tower. Unusual arches
5 Entrance to Saxon crypt
6 Transitional Norman work
7 Screen or pulpitum
8 Choir. Fine carving
9 Architecture changes
10 St Wilfrid's chapel
11 Great east window
12 Chapel of the Holy Spirit
13 Chapter house
14 Stairs to famous library
15 Norman south doorway

People: St Wilfrid, the great arbitrator between the two expressions of the Christian Faith in Saxon England—Celtic and Roman. Linked also with Chichester. The 'Star of the Saxon Church'. St Willibrord (a pupil of St Wilfrid) became a missionary in the Netherlands. James I granted important Charters to the town and minster. The founders of neighbouring Fountains Abbey worshipped here on Christmas Day 1132. Both a cathedral and parish church.

The minster here was established very early on. In St Wilfrid's day the church was said to be one of the foremost stone buildings in Europe. The shrine of this saint attracted many pilgrims in the Middle Ages. The nightly custom of setting the watch has continued for over a thousand years—at 9 p.m. the city hornblower sounds the horn in the market place. Colourful St Wilfrid Procession, early August.

ROCHESTER, Cathedral Church of Christ and the Blessed Virgin Mary

Founded as a cathedral in 604.
Diocese: West Kent, parts of London.
Note especially: Norman work onwards. Norman carving round west door. Crypt and graffiti—wall scratchings.

This diocese is one of the oldest in the country. A line marking the apse of the Saxon church can be seen just inside the west door. The Benedictine monastery was well established by the Normans. William of Perth, a baker murdered by his servant here in Rochester whilst *en route* for the Holy Land, was buried in the cathedral. His shrine attracted many pilgrims whose gifts swelled the funds for further building.

ST ALBANS, Cathedral and Abbey Church of St Alban

Became a cathedral in 1877. One of the foremost abbeys of England. Second longest medieval church.
Diocese: Most of Hertfordshire and Bedfordshire.
Note especially: All of it! Saxon work. Styles of all medieval periods, especially Norman. Central tower (plate 5). Medieval wall paintings. Shrine of Britain's first Christian martyr. One of the largest and finest brasses. Watching loft. Rood screen.
People: Alban, a Roman citizen of nearby Verulamium, converted to the Christian Faith by a fugitive priest and martyred on this hill (*c.* 209). Nicholas Breakspeare was refused admission to the Benedictine monastery as a novice— the only Englishman to become Pope (Adrian IV 1154).

Matthew Paris, 13th century chronicler-monk, a notable historian.

Unlike most of the larger cathedrals, St Albans Abbey is also a parish church. At the dissolution of the monastery it was purchased from the Crown for £400. As a lively parish church and cathedral it continues to attract thousands of visitors. The International Organ Festival, founded in recent years, has an ever greater world-wide appeal, since there is an exceptionally fine organ here. At St Albanstide in June the annual Rose Service in honour of the patron saint is a unique and colourful occasion.

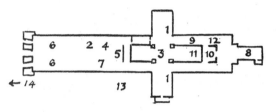

ST ALBANS CATHEDRAL

	7	Decorated Gothic work
	8	Lady Chapel
1	Saxon work	
2	Norman pillars	9 Ramryge Chantry Chapel
3	Norman tower	10 Shrine of Saint Alban
4	Wall paintings	11 High Altar. Screen
5	Nave altar. Rood screen	12 Watching loft
6	Early English work	13 Site of cloisters
		14 Abbey gateway

ST ASAPH, Cathedral Church of St Asaph

Probably founded in early 6th century.

Diocese: Denbighshire, Flintshire, parts of Caernarvonshire, Merionethshire and Montgomeryshire.

Note especially: Fine cruciform shape. The Greyhound Stone. 13th century effigy of a bishop. East window. Variety of styles.

People: In the 6th century Saint Kentigern placed Asaph, a disciple of his, in charge of the monastery here. He died in 596 and his body was venerated for many years. Parliamentary soldiers used the cathedral as a stable in the Civil War. Dr Morgan, famous for his translation of the Bible into Welsh, is commemorated by a fine national monument north of the church.

St Asaph is reputedly the smallest cathedral in England and Wales and indeed one of the oldest.

ST DAVID'S, Cathedral Church of St David

Founded as a cathedral probably in early 6th century.

Diocese: Pembrokeshire, Cardiganshire and Carmarthenshire.

Note especially: Norman arches. Unique nave ceiling in Irish oak. Rood screen. St David's shrine (remains)—casket containing his bones. Celtic remains. Ruins of Bishop's Palace (plate 4).

People: St David, Dewi, Patron Saint of Wales. 6th century bishop. Bishop Gower (1328-47) buried here also. He was once Chancellor of Oxford University and Lord High Chancellor of England.

From the earliest days of its foundation in St David's time, the cathedral, set within a hollow, has suffered damage in war and not least from fire and even earth tremor. This may be the reason for the 'leaning' pillars in the nave. Considerable restoration took place in the last century. A beautiful setting in this rugged corner of the Pembrokeshire coast. An inspiring place of pilgrimage and the cradle of the Christian faith in Wales.

ST EDMUNDSBURY, Cathedral Church of St James, Bury St Edmunds

Became a cathedral in 1913.

Diocese: Most of Suffolk. Called the Diocese of St Edmunds-bury and Ipswich.

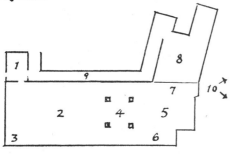

ST EDMUNDSBURY CATHEDRAL

1 New porch	6 New Lady Chapel
2 Nave	7 New chapel (Magna Carta)
3 Susanna window	8 Proposed extension
4 New central tower	9 Cloister walk
5 New choir	10 Abbey of St Edmund—ruins
	11 Fine Norman tower

Note especially: Perpendicular nave. New eastern end. Susanna window. Abbey ruins. Superb Norman tower south of cathedral.

People: St Edmund, king and martyr at the hands of invading Vikings (870). Many notable abbots of the great medieval monastery. Famous scholars. The barons of Magna Carta met here in 1214 to prepare the document. John Wastell, one of the greatest of church architect/builders of the late 15th century.

The shrine of St Edmund of East Anglia was destroyed together with the immense abbey, after the dissolution of the monasteries by Henry VIII. The cathedral is one of the original parish churches built near the monastery for the use of the townsfolk. The town's motto is *Shrine of the King, Cradle of the Law.*

SALISBURY, Cathedral Church of the Blessed Virgin Mary

New cathedral started in 1220. Consecrated 1258 (Diocese 1078, Sherborne 705).

Diocese: A large part of Wiltshire. Dorset.

Note especially: All of it! The 'unity' of the architecture throughout (Early English). The loftiest spire (plate 1). The

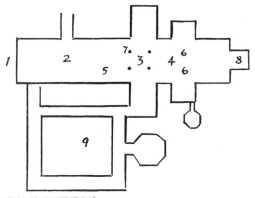

SALISBURY CATHEDRAL

1	West front	5	St Osmund's shrine
2	Nave	6	Strainer arches
3	Central tower. Spire	7	Bending column
4	Choir	8	Lady Chapel
		9	Cloisters

close. Ancient clock. (*cf.* Wells). Tombs. Monuments. Bending column. Lady Chapel. Shrine of St Osmond with 'healing holes'. Chapter house and cloisters.

People: Osmond completed the first cathedral at Old Sarum. He was a learned priest who came with William the Conqueror in 1066. There were no monks at Salisbury since the cathedral was served by a body of canons, special priests forming a chapter.

The original cathedral was at Old Sarum on a hill a short distance away. This cathedral is at 'New Sarum'. The familiar view across the river Avon, of this cathedral with its soaring spire, has been immortalised in the paintings of John Constable. The wonderful close is the largest in the country.

SHEFFIELD, Cathedral Church of St Peter and St Paul
Became a cathedral in 1914.

Diocese: A large part of the West Riding of Yorkshire.

Note especially: Considerable modern extension in keeping with the late Gothic core. Many fine monuments and memorials. Chapter house with sculpture and stained glass. New lantern tower.

A church of ancient origin founded in the 12th century 'in the open space by the river Sheaf'. The settlement has grown into a great industrial city and the story of this 'City of Steel' is told in the stained glass windows of the new chapter house.

SOUTHWARK, Cathedral and Collegiate Church of St Saviour and St Mary Overie
Became a cathedral in 1905.

Diocese: Parts of London and Kent, parts of east and west Surrey.

Note especially: Retro-choir. Numerous memorials and chapels. High Altar stone screen. 16th and 17th century furnishings. Harvard chapel. Several notable people are commemorated here, including William Shakespeare whose Globe Theatre was nearby on the south bank of the Thames, and John Gower also one of the earliest English poets.

St Mary 'Overie' probably means 'over the water', i.e. across the river from the City of London. The foundation dates from Saxon times and the priory was re-established in the early 12th century as a daughter community in the very important Winchester diocese. Today it is a parish church cathedral. Notice 13th century remains of the London Palace of the Bishops of Winchester.

SOUTHWELL, Cathedral and Collegiate Church of the Blessed Virgin Mary

Became a cathedral in 1884.

Diocese: Most of Nottinghamshire.

Note especially: Roman remains. Norman nave. Stone screen with many carved heads. Chapter house with unique carvings, the 'Leaves of Southwell'. Ruins of the archbishop's palace.

In late Saxon times this church became a minster under York Minster and, although it became a cathedral less than a hundred years ago, it has always been the parish church here. It has been called 'the Village Cathedral'.

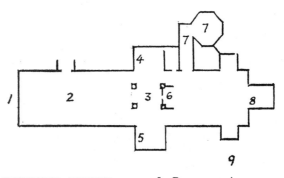

	SOUTHWELL MINSTER	5	Roman paving
		6	Screen or pulpitum
1	West front	7	Chapter house and
2	Nave		approach—famous 'Leaves'
3	Central tower	8	Sedilia
4	Saxon remains	9	Palace ruins

TRURO, Cathedral Church of St Mary

Diocese: Founded in 1877 (cathedral started 1880). Covers Cornwall, Isles of Scilly, two parishes in Devon.

Note especially: High altar reredos. 250 ft. high central tower. Many features which are good examples of the Gothic Revival. St Mary's Aisle (early 16th century).

It has been said that here is 'a little of France in Cornwall'. The county does have an affinity with Brittany across the Channel and the west front here bears, in several respects, a very marked resemblance to those of French cathedrals. A cathedral built 'in the street' in the fashion of the Continent. The Cathedral Church was at St Germans until the 11th century.

WAKEFIELD, Cathedral Church of All Saints

Became a cathedral in 1888.

Diocese: Parts of the north and south divisions of the West Riding of Yorkshire.

Note especially: Various styles of architecture. A large town church, mainly perpendicular with extension work of the beginning of this century. Interesting carvings in choir. Nave windows.

This church has been through various stages of building from its early history in Saxon times, through the Norman period and throughout the Middle Ages. In the early 1300s the original central Norman tower fell down. Today the buttressed tower has a fine crocketted spire reaching to a height of nearly 250 ft.

WELLS, Cathedral Church of St Andrew

Cathedra of first bishop here in 909. The Bishop of Bath

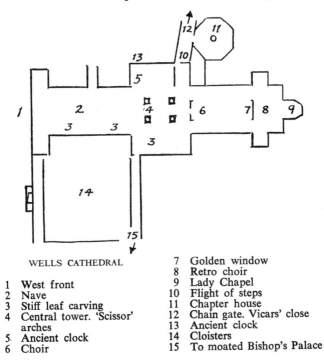

WELLS CATHEDRAL

1 West front
2 Nave
3 Stiff leaf carving
4 Central tower. 'Scissor' arches
5 Ancient clock
6 Choir
7 Golden window
8 Retro choir
9 Lady Chapel
10 Flight of steps
11 Chapter house
12 Chain gate. Vicars' close
13 Ancient clock
14 Cloisters
15 To moated Bishop's Palace

and Wells mid 13th century onwards.

Diocese: Almost the whole of Somerset.

Note especially: All of it! Unique setting. West front. Stiff leaf carvings on capitals. 'Scissor' arches (plate 14). Chapter house and its approach. Ancient clock. Vicars' Close—the oldest complete inhabited street. Moated bishop's palace.

People: Bishop Thomas Ken, one of the famous 'seven bishops who saved England', imprisoned in the Tower of London but later proved not guilty in their stand against the King and released (1688). A saintly, highly respected man. Writer of some famous hymns.

This cathedral, with the Mendip Hills close at hand, has a particularly peaceful and beautiful setting. The Vicars' Choral who deputised for the canons (no monks here) during the Middle Ages had their own community life and many of the ancient buildings associated with them still remain intact and are still in use. The first 'all English' cathedral and reputedly one of the foremost in architectural importance. The restoration of the unique and beautiful West front is a great burden and responsibility.

WINCHESTER, Cathedral Church of the Holy Trinity, St Peter, St Paul and St Swithun

Cathedral founded in mid 7th century (cathedra originally at Dorchester in Oxfordshire—Diocese 676).

Diocese: Most of Hampshire, the Channel Islands.

Note especially: All of it! Perpendicular nave. Norman transept. Font. Many chantry chapels. Wall painting (plate 17). Modern shrine of St Swithun. The Winchester Madonna. High altar screen. Choir-stalls. Bones of Saxon kings.

People: Winchester was once England's capital so many notable people are associated with the city and cathedral. Alfred the Great was probably taught by Swithun, the famous bishop and saint. An event associated with this saint after his death gave rise to the familiar notions concerning the wet English summer! The body of King William Rufus was buried here after his sudden death from an arrow in the New Forest (1100). William Walker, a diver, 'with his own hands' drained and consolidated the marshy foundations of the cathedral early this century. The writer Jane Austen is buried here.

The attraction here in the Middle Ages was St Swithun's tomb, visited by thousands of pilgrims. From King Alfred's time onwards the spirit of education and art was a mark of the monastery here. The tradition of learning has continued and there have been many scholars and preachers connected with this great cathedral, the longest medieval church.

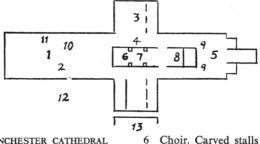

WINCHESTER CATHEDRAL
1 Nave
2 William of Wykeham's chantry
3 Norman north transept
4 Holy Sepulchre Chapel. Wall paintings
5 Shrine of Saint Swithun
6 Choir. Carved stalls
7 Central tower
8 High Altar screen
9 Various chantry chapels
10 Tournai marble font
11 Tomb of Jane Austen
12 Site of cloisters
13 Site of chapter house

WORCESTER, Cathedral Church of Christ and the Blessed Virgin Mary

Founded as a cathedral about 680.

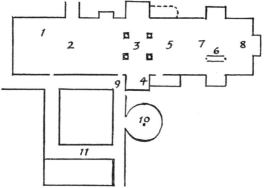

WORCESTER CATHEDRAL

1 Transitional Norman work
2 Nave
3 Central tower
4 Entrance to Norman crypt
5 Choir
6 Prince Arthur's chantry
7 Tomb of King John
8 Lady Chapel
9 Cloisters
10 Chapter house
11 Ceiling carving—'Jesse Tree'

Diocese: Most of Worcestershire, parts of Gloucestershire, Herefordshire and Staffordshire.
Note especially: Norman crypt. Prince Arthur's Chantry. Misericords. Earliest Perpendicular central tower (plate 11). Variety of architectural styles. Monastic ruins.
People: St Wulfstan, popular saint of the Midland church, was the only Saxon bishop to keep his post after the Norman Conquest. The tomb of King John, complete with its ancient effigy, stands before the high altar. Henry VII's son, Prince Arthur, is also commemorated here.

A Benedictine monastery was founded here in the 10th century by St Oswald. Extensive building and restoration over the years. Associated with Sir Edward Elgar and the world famous Three Choirs Festival.

YORK MINSTER, Cathedral Church of St Peter

Founded as a cathedral in the early 7th century (627).
Diocese: Whole of East Riding of Yorkshire. Parts of the other ridings.
Note especially: All of it! Various Gothic styles. Early English lancet windows—'The Five Sisters', with *grisaille* glass. Other medieval stained glass, including the oldest piece. Chapter house.

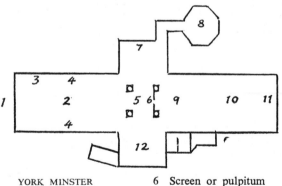

YORK MINSTER	6 Screen or pulpitum
1 West front	7 Five Sisters window
2 Wide and high nave	8 Chapter house
3 Oldest fragment of stained glass	9 Choir
	10 High altar
4 Fine stained glass windows	11 Lady Chapel. Great east window
5 Central tower. Vast crossing	12 South transept

People: King Edwin, baptised by Bishop Paulinus, later founded the original church on this site. Wilfred (*cf.* Chichester and Ripon) was once bishop. King Edward III and Philippa of Hainault married here (1328). Archbishop Scrope murdered by order of King Henry IV in 1405 because of a rebellious act. Duke of Kent married Miss Katherine Worsley (1961).

Built on the site of the Roman headquarters where Constantine was proclaimed Christian emperor (306), the Minster is a truly massive building conveying a unique feeling of spaciousness, more so than any other cathedral of the Middle Ages. Although massive in concept it appears that the Minster has had to fight for survival in recent years during which considerable restoration, strengthening and cleaning has taken place to save it from collapse.

Roman Catholic cathedrals

The medieval cathedrals of England and Wales were, of course, built when Roman Catholicism was the established religion, although they are now Anglican places of worship. There are, however, several cathedrals which were founded in the middle of the last century, after the lifting of the restrictions on Roman Catholicism in Britain.

The dates of the foundations of the Roman Catholic cathedrals in England and Wales are as follows:
1850 Birmingham, Clifton (Bristol), Newcastle, Liverpool, London (Westminster), Menevia (Wrexham), Northampton, Nottingham, Plymouth, Salford (Lancs.), Shrewsbury, Southwark (also London), 1878 Leeds, Middlesbrough, 1882 Portsmouth, 1916 Cardiff, 1917 Brentwood (Essex), 1924 Lancaster, 1966 Brighton/Arundel.

The two most famous Roman Catholic cathedrals are Westminster in London and the new cathedral in Liverpool. **Westminster Cathedral** was built at the turn of the century and is very un-English really, with marble and mosaic decoration. The project is proving somewhat expensive to complete. Over twelve million bricks have been used in the building.

When one compares the new Anglican cathedral at Coventry with the new **Liverpool** Roman Catholic one, the former appears almost conventional and traditional. The latter is basically circular and built of steel and concrete with an imposing central tower, a sixteen-sided lantern tower which perhaps reminds one a little of the fourteenth century Octagon and lantern at Ely. The exterior walls at Liverpool are faced with stone. The interior is bathed in light of various hues, the focal point being, of course, the central altar with its covering or baldacchino of aluminium tubing. Directly above this is the lantern of stained glass windows John Piper worked here as well as at Anglican Coventry. The cathedtal city of Liverpool, with its two massive cathedrals, has an impressive and unique sky-line.

In the summer of 1973 the new cathedral church in a modern style was consecrated at **Clifton**, Bristol, after the very short period of three years in building. Dedicated to Ss. Peter and Paul, it replaces the old 19th century Pro-cathedral. Its imaginative and impressive design is based on a hexagon and equilateral triangles with some splendid modern craftsmanship.

13. FURTHER READING

The Cathedrals of England Harry Batsford and Charles Fry (Batsford)

The Cathedrals of England Alec Clifton-Taylor (Thames and Hudson)

English Cathedrals John Harvey (Batsford)

English Cathedrals in Colour C. L. S. Linnell and A. F. Kersting (Batsford)

The English Cathedral through the Centuries G. H. Cook (Phoenix House)

Looking at Cathedrals Nicholas Taylor (BBC Publications)

The Cathedral Builders Jean Gimpel. Trans. from the French (Evergreen Profile Books)

Discovering Stained Glass John Harries (Shire)

Discovering Wall Paintings E. Clive Rouse (Shire)

FOR YOUNG PEOPLE

Churches and Cathedrals H. and R. Leacroft (Puffin)

Churches and Cathedrals Richard Bowood (Ladybird)

Let's Explore Series (on individual cathedrals) David Pepin (Individual cathedrals and Spectrum Publications)

Cathedral, The Story of its Construction David Macaulay (Collins)

INDEX TO CATHEDRALS

Some titles available in the 'Discovering' series

*From your bookseller or from Shire Publications Ltd.,
Cromwell House, Church Street, Princes Risborough,
Aylesbury, Bucks., U.K.*

Printed by C. I. Thomas & Sons (Haverfordwest) Ltd.,
Press Buildings, Merlins Bridge, Haverfordwest, Pembs.